100 GREATS

NORTHAMPTONSHIRE
COUNTY CRICKET CLUB

David Steele in action.

100 NORTHAMPTONSHIRE

GREATS

COUNTY CRICKET CLUB

WRITTEN BY
ANDREW RADD

TEMPUS

First published 2001
Copyright © Andrew Radd, 2001

Tempus Publishing Limited
The Mill, Brimscombe Port,
Stroud, Gloucestershire, GL5 2QG

ISBN 0 7524 2195 6

Typesetting and origination by
Tempus Publishing Limited
Printed in Great Britain by
Midway Colour Print, Wiltshire

Present and forthcoming cricket titles from Tempus Publishing:

0 7524 2166 2	A False Stroke of Genius: The Wayne Larkins Story	John Wallace	£12.99
0 7524 0792 9	Glamorgan County Cricket Club	Andrew Hignell	£9.99
0 7524 1137 3	Glamorgan County Cricket Club II	Andrew Hignell	£9.99
0 7524 1879 3	Glamorgan CCC: 100 Greats	Andrew Hignell	£9.99
0 7524 2182 4	Glamorgan CCC: Classics	Andrew Hignell	£12.00
0 7524 1876 9	Hampshire County Cricket Club	N. Jenkinson, D. Allen & A. Renishaw	£9.99
0 7524 2188 3	Hampshire CCC: 100 Greats	N. Jenkinson, D. Allen & A. Renishaw	£12.00
0 7524 2167 0	Lord's: Cathedral of Cricket (hb)	Stephen Green	£25.00
0 7524 1871 8	Kent County Cricket Club	William Powell	£9.99
0 7524 1864 5	Leicestershire County Cricket Club	Dennis Lambert	£9.99
0 7524 2175 1	Leicestershire CCC: 100 Greats	Dennis Lambert	£12.00
0 7524 2195 6	Northamptonshire CCC: 100 Greats	Andrew Radd	£12.00
0 7524 1638 3	The Scarborough Cricket Festival	William Powell	£9.99
0 7524 1585 9	Somerset County Cricket Club	Somerset Cricket Museum	£9.99
0 7524 2178 6	Somerset CCC: 100 Greats	Eddie Lawrence	£12.00
0 7524 2192 1	Sussex County Cricket Club	John Wallace	£10.99
0 7524 1885 8	Varsity Cricket	William Powell	£9.99
0 7524 2180 8	Warwickshire CCC: 100 Greats	Robert Brooke	£12.00
0 7524 1834 3	Worcestershire County Cricket Club	Les Hatton	£9.99
0 7524 2194 8	Worcestershire CCC: 100 Greats	Les Hatton	£12.00
0 7524 0756 2	Yorkshire County Cricket Club	Mick Pope	£9.99
0 7524 2179 4	Yorkshire CCC: 100 Greats	Mick Pope & Paul Dyson	£12.00

PREFACE

The late Lew Grade – an even more successful entertainment impresario than Ken Turner – once remarked: 'All my shows are great. Some of them are bad. But they are all great.' Not all of this book's subjects were great players, but I would contend that they all qualify as great cricketers in the broadest sense. In the story of a club like Northamptonshire, which has known more years of adversity than prosperity, the generous, if portly, Lord Lilford is as significant a figure as the explosive, self-confident and richly-talented Allan Lamb.

Selectors are, by tradition, reviled figures, and I do not expect to avoid the wrath of the West Stand for my choice . Lilford and Tommy Askham might, perhaps, be regarded as the wild cards in the pack. Jack Mercer may only have appeared once in first-class cricket for the County, but for his contribution to Northamptonshire over many years he gets in ahead of, for example, Dennis Lillee or Kapil Dev – both all-time greats on the international scene, but short-stay residents at Wantage Road.

Objectivity is never easy when it comes to boyhood heroes or close friends. Both categories are represented here, and I can't help feeling pangs of remorse at the non-inclusion of two valued chums, Alastair Storie and Gareth Smith, who provided a pair of memorable County Ground moments in the 1980s; a century on debut against Hampshire and a second-ball dismissal of Sunil Gavaskar respectively. At the same time, it would be wonderful to think that one or more of the youngsters who formed the initial intake of Northamptonshire's academy in the autumn of 2000 might earn a place in a similar volume produced in, say, twenty years' time.

Statistical note:

All of the career statistics are correct to 1 April 2001, and refer to performances for Northamptonshire only.

Statistics in normal text denote first-class cricket since 1905. Those in italics show a player's record in one-day competitions – Sunday/National League, Gillette Cup/NatWest Trophy and Benson&Hedges Cup. Figures in brackets indicate matches for Northamptonshire between 1896, when the club entered the Second-Class Counties (later Minor Counties) competition, and promotion to first-class status after the 1904 season.

Acknowledgements

My grateful thanks go to many individuals who have helped with the preparation of this book: to Dennis Brookes and Stephen Coverdale for reading the manuscript and offering a number of helpful suggestions, and to the latter for writing the foreword; to James Howarth and everyone at Tempus Publishing; to John Watson, Ian Davidson of the *Northamptonshire Evening Telegraph* and Northamptonshire CCC for providing the photographs; to Matthew Engel for his interest in the project and his views – some of which I have heeded – on which players should get the nod; to Brian Reynolds, for additional anecdotes and the best beef curry in Kettering; and to the staff of the Central Library in Northampton who have always coped cheerfully and patiently with my enquiries and requests for information.

This book is intended primarily to celebrate achievements on the field, but it's impossible to write even a preface on the subject of Northamptonshire cricket without mentioning the late Ken Turner, secretary from 1958 to 1985 and one of a handful of genuine visionaries in the post-war English game. I can almost hear his comments on one or two of my selections, suggesting that if I had any senses to begin with I've certainly taken leave of them now. That said, I would still like to dedicate this volume to the memory of 'KCT' – one of the most fascinating men I have had the privilege of knowing.

Andrew Radd
Northampton
February 2001

Key:
The letters at the top of the page refer to the following batting or bowling styles:

RHB – right-handed batsman
LHB – left-handed batsman
OB – off-break bowler
SLA – slow left arm spin
RFM – right-arm fast medium
RF – right-arm fast
LF – left-arm fast
LM – left-arm medium pace
RM – right-arm medium pace
LB – leg-break bowler
WK – wicketkeeper

FOREWORD

It is a strange existence. Apart from politics, no other form of employment exposes its exponents to such public and stark scrutiny on a daily basis. For nearly six months each year, from the chills of mid-April to the autumn leaves of late September, cricketers perform, succeed and fail. Their achievements and disasters, once chronicled in the late edition of the evening 'paper or scrutinised at the breakfast table, are now, in this electronic age, instantly available. A New Zealander can learn that a wicket has fallen at Northampton even before the unfortunate batsman has completed his walk back to the pavilion. Sometimes described as a circus, county cricket more often appears to be a goldfish bowl. But the nature of the game, its idiosyncrasies and uncertainties, help forge and develop characters and personalities.

Over a period of time, the cricketer's temperament, his strengths and weaknesses, become apparent even to those who have rarely – if ever – seen him perform in the flesh. Followers from afar, for whom county cricket has an integral part to play in the rhythm and pattern of each passing year, somehow feel they 'know' the characters who grace the cricketing stage season after season. Mental images are formed, helped by the occasional photograph or feature article, or more recently by television coverage, which has become ever-more intrusive. But there remains a mystery, sometimes even a mystique, about the vast majority of professional cricketers.

Down the years, Northamptonshire have had real personalities, not stereotypes. There have been the cantankerous, the argumentative and the rebellious; a few artists and many artisans; the usual crop of underachievers and occasionally some tragic figures. There have also been the truly great players, inspiring leaders and individuals whose lives have been devoted to the County. Such men have enlivened, enlightened and enriched the game of cricket.

Northamptonshire's story is remarkable in itself. The smallest first-class county, competing against others with far greater playing and commercial resources, its presence at such an exalted level is seen by many as an anachronism. Until relatively recently the County Ground was uninspiring and inhospitable. But through the trials and tribulations, perhaps as a result of the adversities endured and overcome, certain characteristics and core values have become ingrained in the typical Northamptonshire cricketer. Quite clearly, the club became more than merely an employer to so many, even those who felt mistreated or let down by it during or at the end of their careers. They may not have enjoyed the glamour, riches and rewards of their fellow professionals in other counties, but Northamptonshire entered their souls. Some stayed long after their playing days, to put something back. Others returned to give service. The vast majority – yes, even the disaffected and disgruntled – have retained links and liaisons with the club.

To single out the greatest cricketers to have represented any county over a long period is an invidious exercise. The price to be paid for subjectivity is the certain knowledge that someone will disagree with the final choices. But one hundred men have been chosen. People who have touched others' emotions, excited and entertained them, occasionally infuriated and saddened them. Together they have all played a part in a story which has never been dull, and often dramatic.

Stephen Coverdale
Chief Executive of Northamptonshire CCC
2001

100 NORTHAMPTONSHIRE GREATS

Hylton Ackerman
Mick Allen
Curtly Ambrose
Keith Andrew
Peter Arnold
Tommy Askham
Rob Bailey
Fred Bakewell
Des Barrick
Bill Barron
Bishan Bedi
Ben Bellamy
Robin Boyd-Moss
Vince Broderick
Dennis Brookes
Freddie Brown
'Beau' Brown
Walter Buswell
David Capel
Bob Carter
'Nobby' Clark
Bob Clarke
Geoff Cook
Nick Cook
Bob Cottam
Arthur Cox
Brian Crump
Kevin Curran
Percy Davis
Winston Davis
Jack & Billy Denton
Mike Dilley
John Dye
William East

Alan Fordham
Jim Griffiths
Roger Harper
Rawlins Hawtin
Matthew Hayden
Bob Haywood
Alan Hodgson
Tom Horton
Fred Jakeman
Ken James
Laurie Johnson
Vallance Jupp
Jim Kingston
Billy Kingston
Anil Kumble
Allan Lamb
Wayne Larkins
David Larter
Albert Lightfoot
Lord Lilford
'Jock' Livingston
Mal Loye
Neil Mallender
Jack Manning
'Tim' Manning
Austin Matthews
Jack Mercer
Colin Milburn
Vernon Murdin
Mushtaq Mohammad
Robert Nelson
Mick Norman
Albert Nutter
Norman Oldfield

Reg Partridge
Tony Penberthy
Charles Pool
Roger Prideaux
Brian Reynolds
David Ripley
David Sales
Sarfraz Nawaz
Malcolm Scott
George Sharp
Charles Smith
Sydney Smith
Alex Snowden
David Steele
Raman Subba Row
Haydn Sully
Paul Taylor
Albert Thomas
George Thompson
Jack Timms
Wilfrid Timms
George Tribe
Frank Tyson
'Tubby' Vials
Roy Virgin
'Fanny' Walden
Jim Watts
'Bumper' Wells
Duncan Wild
Peter Willey
Richard Williams
Claud Woolley

The top 20, who appear here in italics, occupy two pages instead of the usual one.

Hylton Ackerman
LHB, 1967-71

Born: Springs, South Africa, 28 April 1947

Batting Career:

M	I	NO	Runs	HS
98	174	10	5182	208
50	*49*	*6*	*1296*	*115**
Ave	**100**	**50**	**ct/st**	
31.59	8	26	89	
30.14	*1*	*8*	*19*	

Bowling Career:

Runs	Wkts	Ave
103	4	25.75
9	*0*	*-*
BB	**5wi**	**10wm**
2-28	-	-
-	*-*	*-*

Early in 1965, secretary Ken Turner received an enthusiastic recommendation from Percy Davis, the former Northamptonshire batting stalwart then coaching in South Africa. A strong seventeen-year-old left-hander by the name of Hylton Ackerman – who had toured England with South African Schoolboys in 1963 – had just taken 108 off Mike Smith's MCC team while playing for Border, and Davis urged his old county to sign the teenager on a long-term contract. In the event, national service prevented Ackerman from making his Northamptonshire debut until 1967, and he qualified for County Championship cricket the following year.

Finding his feet during the 1968 campaign, the young man from the mining town of Springs in the Transvaal proceeded to top 1,000 first-class runs in each of the next three summers. In 1970 he scored a career-best 208 against Leicestershire at Grace Road, and also registered Northamptonshire's first century in the newfangled Sunday League with 115 not out against Kent at Dover, in what was the competition's second season.

How spectators, at Wantage Road and elsewhere, would have relished the sight of an in-form Ackerman plundering opening attacks with his sometime flatmate and fellow roisterer, Colin Milburn. The latter's tragic car accident in May 1969 killed off that mouth-watering prospect, much to the detriment of the county game which at that time needed all the entertainers it could find.

South Africa's sporting isolation cost Ackerman his chance to impress in the Test arena, although he offered a glimpse of what might have been in hitting 112 for a World XI against Australia – Dennis Lillee, Graham McKenzie *et al* – at Brisbane in 1971/72. He also enjoyed the considerable, albeit belated, satisfaction of seeing his son 'H.D.' bat his way into the Proteas side in 1998.

Ackerman's Northamptonshire career ended when he decided not to return to England in 1972. However, he continued to turn out in South African domestic cricket, mostly for Western Province, for another ten years. In the year 2000, after establishing a formidable reputation as a coach of young cricketers at the Plascon Academy, he was voted onto his country's national selection panel.

Mick Allen
RHB and SLA, 1956-63

Born: Bedford, 7 January 1933
Died: Lancaster, 6 October 1995
Batting Career:

M	I	NO	Runs	HS
155	183	40	1418	59
Ave	100	50	ct/st	
9.91	-	2	139	

Bowling Career:

Runs	Wkts	Ave
9148	424	21.57

BB	5wi	10wm
8-48	20	3

Few players have made as spectacular a start in Northamptonshire colours as Micky Allen in May 1956. An injury to Vince Broderick opened up a first-team opportunity for the twenty-three-year-old slow left-armer, who had been chosen in the same Public Schools representative side to play the Combined Services at Lord's as Colin Cowdrey and Micky Stewart. But on his debut, against Worcestershire at Northampton, he wasn't called upon to send down a single over, having to content himself with scoring 51 in a rain-affected draw.

Next day, the team headed up to Trent Bridge to tackle Nottinghamshire, and Allen made up for his inactivity in the previous fixture by claiming 8-88 from 20.4 overs on a blameless pitch, actually taking the last eight wickets to fall after Frank Tyson had snapped up the first two.

His promise as a batsman remained unfulfilled, but as an accurate, economical and hard-working bowler, and an excellent close fielder, he earned a regular place in the County side for seven seasons. Allen's flight was rarely extravagant and his turn rarely prodigious. However, he could exploit helpful conditions to telling effect, and made himself into a thoroughly useful man to have around.

In 1957 he appeared in all twenty-eight Championship games and harvested 77 wickets at 15.90, forming a lethal spin force with the two Australians, George Tribe and Jack Manning. Between the three of them they accounted for 305 batsmen that summer, helping Northamptonshire to runners-up spot in the table behind Surrey. Allen also weighed in with 30 catches.

Leg-spinner Peter Watts denied him his first-team spot for the latter part of 1959, and he also lost out to Malcolm Scott during 1961, despite a destructive performance (8-48 in the first innings and 13-98 in the match) against Derbyshire at Northampton in May. Only David Larter bettered Allen's 76 Championship wickets for Northamptonshire in 1962, but by the end of the following season he was well and truly out of the picture once again, and this time the club chose to release him.

Allen was able to prolong his career for a further three summers by joining Derbyshire, and retired in 1966 with exactly 500 first-class wickets to his credit.

Curtly Ambrose

LHB and RF, 1989-96

Born: Swetes Village, Antigua 21 September 1963				
Batting Career:				
M	**I**	**NO**	**Runs**	**HS**
78	96	26	1100	78
95	*44*	*16*	*404*	*48*
Ave	**100**	**50**	**ct/st**	
15.71	-	2	38	
14.43	*-*	*-*	*30*	
Bowling Career:				
Runs	**Wkts**	**Ave**		
6552	318	20.60		
2549	*115*	*22.17*		
BB	**5wi**	**10wm**		
7-44	20	4		
4-7	*-*	*-*		

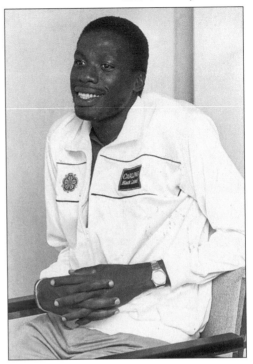

The great Antiguan fast bowler, who made such an emotional farewell to Test cricket at The Oval in 2000, in turn delighted and infuriated Northamptonshire supporters during his five summers with the club. 'Is he really trying? Is he really interested?' asked West Standers from time to time; then a stump would fly, a rip-snorting lifter slap into David Ripley's gloves or a low slip catch settle in his big hands with deceptive ease and Ambrose had provided the answer.

Northamptonshire showed remarkable prescience in signing him during the winter of 1987/88, before his West Indies debut. Stephen Coverdale and Brian Reynolds, chief executive and Cricket Development Officer respectively, had watched him bowl in a Lancashire League game at Heywood and, Coverdale's observation that 'He looks like a pipe-cleaner' notwithstanding, offered him terms.

Chosen for the Windies' 1988 tour of England, he shared the overseas player duties at Northampton with Winston Davis in both 1989 and 1990, returning in 1992 to play a pivotal role in the NatWest Trophy triumph. His spell of 4-7 from 8.3 overs to dispose of Yorkshire in the second round ranks as one of the outstanding bowling efforts for Northamptonshire in nearly four decades of limited-overs cricket.

Ambrose's performances – and personality – dominated the Wantage Road scene to a remarkable degree in 1994. His late arrival in April, leaving Coverdale to twiddle his thumbs at the airport, prompted an angry response from supporters and team-mates alike. By September, however, with 77 wickets at 14.45 to his name, not to mention a match-winning knock of 78 at Taunton, he could do no wrong.

The big man's final summer with the club, 1996, found him as effective as ever in the matches he was able to play, but fitness problems ruled him out for half the programme and it came as no great surprise when the committee opted to look elsewhere for 1997. Ambrose departed with his popularity around the County Ground probably greater than ever; it was just a pity that his famed aversion to the media prevented him sharing his views on an eventful stint at Northampton with the club's followers.

Keith Andrew
RHB and WK, 1953-66

Born: Oldham, 15 December 1929				
Batting Career:				
M	**I**	**NO**	**Runs**	**HS**
351	428	150	3830	76
9	*6*	*2*	*15*	*6**
Ave	**100**	**50**	**ct/st**	
13.77	-	3	653/157	
3.75	*-*	*-*	*6*	

Bowling Career:		
Runs	**Wkts**	**Ave**
31	2	15.50
BB	**5wi**	**10wm**
2-9	-	-

Jack Jennings, Northamptonshire's durable physiotherapist and father-confessor, put it succinctly: 'If Keith (Andrew) fell out with anyone, he must have been driven to it.' This explains the Lancastrian's abiding personal popularity at Wantage Road and beyond, just as his prowess behind the stumps and tactical shrewdness explain the high esteem in which he is still held as a wicketkeeper and captain. Like 'Tubby' Vials more than half a century before, 'K.V.' came desperately close to winning the County Championship with a side possessing rather more in the way of solid professionalism than eye-catching glamour.

Andrew's acquisition was another scouting feather in the cap of Jock Livingston, who had spotted him playing for Werneth in the Central Lancashire League. The powers that be at Old Trafford initially refused Northamptonshire permission to approach the young 'keeper, but at a selection committee meeting in May 1952 Livingston was reported to be 'arranging things quietly.' British Timken's help was enlisted, and in Andrew the firm was getting itself a bright young man with an engineering background

as well as furnishing the County with another talented cricketer. After national service in the army he made his Northamptonshire debut in 1953, and qualified for the Championship the following year.

Andrew himself has written (in his valuable *Handbook of Cricket*, published in 1989) that there is more to wicketkeeping than 'being simply a straight first slip with gloves on, trained mainly as an acrobat.' His excellence, day in and day out, made him a role model for a generation of English stumpers, and at the end of the 2000 season he remained more than 100 dismissals ahead of David Ripley, his nearest challenger in Northamptonshire's all-time list. The record book offers further evidence; a tally of 90 victims in 1962, including seven catches in an innings against his native Lancashire, and 2,132 runs scored by the opposition without a bye being conceded in 1965.

That he made only 2 Test appearances, more than eight years apart, probably owes more to a career batting average of 13.77 than any deficiencies in his glovework. Godfrey Evans, Jim Parks and John Murray were all regarded as better bets for a few runs down the order. Andrew passed fifty only three times in his 351 matches for the County.

But Northamptonshire were the principal beneficiaries of this selectorial policy, especially

Waiting for a nick – Keith Andrew behind the stumps against Middlesex in the 1960s. Peter Parfitt is the batsman.

after he succeeded Raman Subba Row as skipper. Frank Tyson has described his old friend and fellow instigator of the Cosmo Social Club as 'absent-minded to the degree that he often forgot what he was saying in mid-sentence,' and claimed that he would 'frequently wander off into cloud-cuckoo-land' developing this or that theory. Ken Turner told the story of discovering Andrew reading *Wisden* in the gents to try and ascertain how the opposition's batsmen usually got out. Whatever his methods, they worked more often than not; from sixteenth place in Subba Row's final season, Northamptonshire climbed to eighth, seventh, third and then a close second in 1965 before slipping back to fifth in Andrew's farewell year. He knew and understood his players, and they in turn responded to him.

For a while, it looked as though Andrew would be returning to the club in an even more exalted capacity. With Turner due to retire as secretary in 1985, after twenty-seven years in harness, the committee needed to find someone of sufficient stature to replace the seemingly irreplaceable. In October 1984, to general acclaim around the County, it was announced that Andrew would be the man. With survival assured on and off the field, thanks in no small measure to Turner's efforts, it was time, said the secretary/manager-elect, for Northamptonshire to forge ahead.

In the event, he had second thoughts about the job without ever getting his feet under the desk. It went instead to Stephen Coverdale, and Andrew served as chief executive of the National Cricket Association from 1986 to 1994. He remains, however, a keen observer of his old county's fortunes, not least through his regular column – blending nostalgia and technical advice with trenchant comment on the current scene – in the *Northampton Chronicle and Echo.*

Keith Andrew (right) *with Ken Turner, in 1984.*

Peter Arnold

RHB, 1951-60

Born: Wellington, New Zealand 16 October 1926				
Batting Career:				
M	**I**	**NO**	**Runs**	**HS**
167	294	13	7420	122
Ave	**100**	**50**	**ct/st**	
26.40	5	42	73	
Bowling Career:				
Runs	**Wkts**	**Ave**		
79	3	26.33		
BB	**5wi**	**10wm**		
1-5	-	-		

When Peter Arnold embarked on the long sea voyage from his native New Zealand to England in 1950, at his own expense, he was backing himself to shine as a county cricketer with Northamptonshire. Half a century later, at the 2000 Annual General Meeting, he completed a four-year term as the club's president. To say that 'Kiwi' has managed to make himself at home in Northampton is to offer the very baldest of understatements.

Recommended by Frank O'Brien, a Christchurch man who represented the County in 1938 and 1939, Arnold created a sufficiently favourable impression to be taken on the staff – despite Vince Broderick's laconic first-day observation that 'you'll never play cricket with a pair of pads like that' – and, after cutting his first-class teeth against Scotland in 1951, he 'arrived' in earnest with 68 on his Championship debut at Old Trafford five weeks later. Significantly, he batted down at number seven in that game. It was only in 1954, with the retirement of 'Buddy' Oldfield, that he was promoted to open with Dennis Brookes,

a position he then occupied for the best part of six seasons.

A good deal of Arnold's subsequent success has been attributed to his short backlift – a particularly useful technical trait in an era of English fast-bowling strength – and his splendid understanding with Brookes between the wickets. His most productive season was 1955, when he notched 1,596 runs with 3 centuries, including a career-best 122 against Somerset at Taunton. He also exceeded 1,000 runs in 1956 and 1958.

He retired, along with Frank Tyson, at the end of 1960, but maintained his interest in the club and in 1978 became the first chairman of Northamptonshire's new cricket sub-committee, established to replace the old selection committee. It was a role he was to fill for fifteen years, through a period of seismic change in the game, and in that capacity he acted as tour manager on the County's first pre-season overseas trip, to KwaZulu Natal in 1992.

Peter Arnold's elevation to the presidency in 1996 was a fitting reward for the efforts of a man with a passionate and unashamedly emotional commitment to Northamptonshire County Cricket Club.

Tommy Askham

RHB and RM, 1914

Born: Wellingborough, 9 September 1896				
Died: Mailly-Maillet Wood, France 21 August 1916				
Batting Career:				
M	I	NO	Runs	HS
5	9	3	83	28*
Ave	100	50	ct/st	
13.83	-	-	-	
Bowling Career:				
Runs	Wkts	Ave		
86	2	43.00		
BB	5wi	10wm		
2-68	-	-		

Glance at the fading team boards inside Wellingborough School's old tea pavilion and you may spot the name of S.T. Askham in the sides of 1912 to 1915 inclusive. He was, according to *Wisden*, 'an exceptional boy cricketer (who) met with astonishing success as a bowler, and is a fine batsman too.' Indeed, he was exceptional enough to play in five Championship games for Northamptonshire in his penultimate year at school, and be awarded a County cap before his eighteenth birthday.

Unfortunately, Askham's penultimate year at school happened to be 1914, and a few hours after the close of play on the second day of his debut match, against Leicestershire at Northampton, Britain declared war on Germany. He had enjoyed his last cricket in peacetime. The youngster remained in Northamptonshire's team for the rest of the season and secured his maiden first-class wicket – William Tyldesley of Lancashire, caught by his fellow Wellingburian, Donald Denton – at Old Trafford. A poignant scorebook entry indeed; bowler and batsman would both die in the war, while the fielder lost part of a leg.

The summer of 1915 was Askham's final fling on The Grove. He set a new school record of 62 wickets at less than 14 runs apiece, and hit 149 against Dulwich. In October he should have gone up to Cambridge University, having won a scholarship. Instead he headed for Colchester to take up a commission in the Suffolk Regiment.

Second-Lieutenant Askham came through his first action without a scratch, but his luck ran out near a straggling wood, named 'P18' from its map reference, in the Albert sector of the Western Front. 'He was given a very difficult task to perform, but he willingly undertook it' reported *The Wellingburian* magazine. 'He led his men right up to the German lines where he fell, urging them on when he himself was wounded. His sergeant went to rescue him but while doing so a second shot hit him in the head and killed him instantly.'

Tommy Askham was nineteen years old when he died. Would he have become an undisputed 'Northamptonshire great' given the opportunity? No-one knows – but he is included here, just in case.

Rob Bailey
RHB and OB, 1982-99

Born: Biddulph, Staffs, 28 October 1963				
Batting Career:				
M	**I**	**NO**	**Runs**	**HS**
336	564	80	20,181	224*
345	*327*	*56*	*10,857*	*145*
Ave	**100**	**50**	**ct/st**	
41.69	44	102	253	
39.07	*9*	*72*	*97*	

Bowling Career:		
Runs	**Wkts**	**Ave**
4,790	112	42.76
1,978	*58*	*34.10*
BB	**5wi**	**10wm**
5-54	2	-
3-23	*-*	*-*

If ever a cricketer seized the day it was Rob Bailey on 29 April 1984. All set for another season in the Second XI, his path to promotion blocked by Northamptonshire's settled top six, the twenty-year-old son of a Staffordshire policeman received the call to deputise for flu victim Richard Williams in the opening Championship match against Warwickshire at Edgbaston. In only his fifth innings in the competition, Bailey made an unbeaten 100 in two-and-a-half hours. He was to remain a fixture in the County side for the next fifteen years, topping 20,000 first-class runs with 44 centuries.

Like Aristotle's model gentleman, 'Bailers' proved himself a thoroughly reliable sort: 'Neither excitable nor highly strung, he speaks and acts straightforwardly. His gait is measured...and his speech unhurried.' He began his career as a hard-hitting number five – 'The Biddulph Blaster' of tabloid legend – but, largely as a result of Robin Boyd-Moss' premature retirement, moved up to number three, and was usually obliged to keep under wraps the natural flair which, had it been given its full rein, would surely have secured him more than 4 Test

appearances. The promise was unquestionably there; at the end of 1984 he became the first, and so far only, Northamptonshire recipient of the Cricket Writers' Club's Young Player of the Year award.

Bailey had an outstanding summer in 1986, notching 1,805 runs at 54.69, including a career-best 224 not out off Glamorgan's bowlers at Swansea. The England selectors eventually turned to him a couple of years later, as a replacement for the injured Allan Lamb in the Fifth Test against the West Indies at The Oval. Bailey made a resolute 43 in the first innings, and might reasonably have anticipated being retained for the following game against Sri Lanka, whose attack would have offered an altogether less physically threatening challenge. He was left out. Consolation came in the shape of a place on that winter's tour to India, but this was cancelled for political reasons. A great many cricketers in his situation would have accepted with alacrity the offer made twelve months later to join the 'rebel' trip to South Africa, but he declined it, still intent on making an England berth his own.

That loyalty was rewarded when the Caribbean beckoned early in 1990. Affable to a fault, he unwillingly found himself a central figure in the major row of the series in Barbados, courtesy of Viv Richards'

Reliable and personable, Rob Bailey was as successful on the field as he was popular off it.

histrionics which led to umpire Lloyd Barker sending Bailey on his way with a highly suspect caught-behind verdict. He scored 42 and 8 in the final Test in Antigua – and that, as far as his international cricket went, was that.

To his credit, Bailey bounced back from this traumatic experience to enjoy his most productive summer with Northamptonshire; a return of 1,987 runs with 7 centuries and an average of 64. In 1991 he became Allan Lamb's vice-captain, and succeeded him as skipper in 1996. His elevation coincided with John Emburey's arrival as chief coach and within a couple of months the new leadership duo had guided the team to the Benson & Hedges Cup final. Defeat at the hands of Lancashire, a poor Championship showing and failure to capitalise on a promising early-August position in the Sunday League made it, ultimately, a frustrating year. Much worse was to follow in 1997, and the qualities admired by Aristotle were suddenly regarded less favourably by Northamptonshire's committee. Bailey lost the captaincy to Kevin Curran.

Professional to a fault, he played on under the new leader in 1998, only to find his Championship place far from secure the following season after a brief spell opening the innings. Convinced that he still had plenty of cricket left in him, Bailey moved to Derbyshire where, to the pleasure of his many remaining friends and admirers in Northampton, his debut summer brought him 'Player of the Year' accolades from both the supporters and his team-mates.

Fred Bakewell

RHB, 1927-36

Born: Walsall, 2 November 1908
Died: Bournemouth, 23 January 1983
Batting Career:

M	I	NO	Runs	HS
227	417	21	13,543	257
Ave	**100**	**50**	**ct/st**	
34.19	29	69	213	

Bowling Career:

Runs	Wkts	Ave
1,263	22	57.40
BB	**5wi**	**10wm**
2-17	-	-

When Aubrey Faulkner, the renowned South African all-rounder and coach, first saw Fred Bakewell bat, he instantly recognised something special, declaring: 'Here is a genius whom I shall leave well alone.' Although not entirely sold on the youngster's method, particularly the pronounced two-shouldered stance, Faulkner was not about to interfere. Bakewell, first introduced to the game in the yard of St John's approved school at Tiffield where the headmaster, Trevor McColl, encouraged the boys to play with cut-down bats and rubber balls, went on score enough runs to impress spectators, critics and even selectors, in a career sufficiently brief to make them wonder subsequently how many he *might* have made.

In 1927, when he was eighteen, the local press began to take an interest in this highly-regarded talent. 'Northamptonshire is very well off for young players of promise, including the Tiffield boy Blakewell,' ran the story in the late, lamented *Northampton Independent*. They even, in time, began to spell his name correctly. Bakewell's County debut came in June 1928 and, his batting apart, he was worth his place as a superb close fielder, blessed with the sharpest of reflexes. During that first season he held eight catches in the match against Essex at Leyton, a tally never bettered for Northamptonshire.

His progress thereafter was rapid and spectacular. He sailed past 1,000 runs in 1929 and 1930, gaining wider recognition in the latter year with a classy 84 against the Australians and a maiden double-century, featuring 30 fours, off Somerset's bowlers at Bath. By 1931 he was an England player, selected for the first two Tests against New Zealand, and they took another look at him a couple of seasons later in the wake of a phenomenal burst of run-scoring for Northamptonshire.

At the start of 1933, the County's highest individual innings was Billy Denton's unbeaten 230, recorded two decades earlier at Leyton. Bakewell promptly set a new mark with 246 against Nottinghamshire, flaying the normally accurate off-spin of Sam Staples to all parts of the County Ground; and in the very next match, with Glamorgan at Swansea, he fared even better, stroking 257 in eight-and-a-quarter hours. Recalled by England to face the West Indies at The Oval in August, Bakewell helped rescue the side from trouble

Left: *Fred Bakewell opens the Northamptonshire innings with Alex Snowden in 1934, and (right) displays the style that brought him runs for county and country.*

at 68-4 with a knock of 107 – 'a sensible, controlled innings' according to *Wisden*. He went to India with Douglas Jardine's MCC party in the winter of 1933/34, and his international appearances ended with two Tests against the 1935 South Africans.

The summer of 1936 found him scoring solidly again, signing off with 241 not out against Derbyshire, the County Champions-elect, at Chesterfield. It was to be his last time at the crease in first-class cricket. The car carrying Reggie Northway, who was driving, and Bakewell home from Queen's Park crashed at Burton Brook Bridge in Leicestershire. Northway, an amateur batsman new to Northamptonshire that season, was killed outright, and Bakewell badly injured. Despite a few hopeful-sounding reports over the next three years, his playing days were over.

Fred Bakewell would, perhaps, have been a major celebrity today, when the 'bad boy' and 'anti-hero' figures reign supreme. Norman Cole has written that he should have starred in *The Blackboard Jungle* or *Angels with Dirty Faces*. Reg Partridge remembered 'Taffy' Thomas, the senior professional when Bakewell came into the team, sitting on the newcomer's bed 'trying to talk some sense into him.'

Predictably, R.C. Robertson-Glasgow – more able than most to empathise with complex personalities – summed him up best: 'He did not bother to hide his love of freedom and company, and he remained the boy who wouldn't touch his cap to the important visitor. He needed a leader-manager, not merely a captain, and it was not all his own fault that he never found one. Neither his own temperament nor external comment could always make him care; but, when his mind and his fortunes were warm, he could have batted with Bradman on not uneven terms.'

Bakewell (who, later in life, lost an eye in another car smash to underline the parallels with Colin Milburn) returned to Wantage Road not long before his death, content to sit unobtrusively in the crowd. 'I didn't want anyone to know I was there' he said.

Des Barrick
RHB and LB, 1949-60

Born: Fitzwilliam, Yorks. 28 April 1926

Batting Career:

M	I	NO	Runs	HS
267	434	56	12,443	211
Ave	**100**	**50**	**ct/st**	
32.91	18	59	103	

Bowling Career:

Runs	Wkts	Ave
2,562	57	44.94
BB	**5wi**	**10wm**
5-71	2	-

Hailing from Fitzwilliam, the Yorkshire mining village which gave the cricketing world Geoffrey Boycott a few years later, Des Barrick was a late developer who only took up the game seriously as a nineteen-year-old. His early reputation was made primarily as a leg-break and googly bowler, but he became one of Northamptonshire's leading run-scorers of the 1950s, and a ripe character to boot. 'One hopes that his natural sense of humour will never disappear; he is a natural comic' wrote Jim Coldham of the former Bevin Boy in 1958.

Finding his way to Wantage Road in June 1949 after convincing interested Yorkshire officials that he was engaged to a Northampton girl (Churchill might have deemed this a 'terminological inexactitude'), Barrick scored an unbeaten 147 against the touring New Zealanders in only his second first-class match. Northamptonshire, delighted at the acquisition of what the committee regarded as a 'ready-made player', had high hopes of him, but he did not command a regular top-order berth until 1952. He broke through then with 1,570 runs, including 211 against Essex at Northampton, sharing a fifth-wicket stand of 347 with Dennis Brookes which was, at the time, a County record for any wicket.

Barrick was also coming to terms with the pecking order in the dressing room. He admitted, many years later, to having once grabbed first use of the one and only bath, usually reserved for the exclusive use of the captain, Freddie Brown. Brookes, the senior professional, proceeded to painstakingly explain the order of seniority, ending his lecture with the observation that 'If there's enough hot water left to wash your big toe, you'll be bloody lucky!'

He made 1,000 runs in six of the eight summers between 1953 and 1960, and displayed his talents further afield on tours to India and Jamaica with the Commonwealth team and Duke of Norfolk's XI respectively. In 1960 he deputised as captain for Raman Subba Row, but injury kept him out of contention at the start of the following season and he parted company with the club in July. Happily, his anecdotes – including the tale of him and Bob Clarke catching the bus home from one of physiotherapist Jack Jennings' pre-season runs – continued to enliven Former Players' Reunions for many years after that.

Born: Herrington, Co. Durham,
26 October 1917

Batting Career:

M	I	NO	Runs	HS
118	196	13	4,751	161*
Ave	**100**	**50**	**ct/st**	
25.96	6	22	98/2	

Bowling Career:

Runs	Wkts	Ave
200	5	40.00
BB	**5wi**	**10wm**
1-1	-	-

Bill Barron was a member of that happy breed who managed to combine professional soccer with first-class cricket, in an era when the former had a season which started and finished rather than occupying the entire year. He played the bulk of his League football – 172 first-team games – for Northampton Town and later turned out for Kettering Town. Having appeared for his native Durham before the Second World War and once for Lancashire immediately afterwards, Northamptonshire was his cricketing county for six seasons.

Barron first caught the eye with a high-class innings of 151 against Surrey at The Oval in June 1946 – the team's seventh post-war Championship game. He struck 17 fours, earned himself a basket of fruit from the club's secretary, Lt-Col Coldwell, and attracted high praise from his captain, Peter Murray-Willis: 'Some of his left-handed strokes on the off-side are brilliant in the extreme, and already he ranks as one of the best left-handers who have played for the County.' Not surprisingly, given his winter occupation, he pepped up the fielding considerably, just as Fanny Walden had done thirty-odd years before, and also tweaked the occasional leg-break.

He passed the 1,000 run mark again in 1947, helping himself to another century off Surrey's attack in Kennington – this time a chanceless 144, against the Bedsers and Alf Gover, out of Northamptonshire's 308 all out. It was, arguably, Barron's finest hour with a cricket bat. He rescued the side from the depths of 39-6 after Gover had snapped up five victims for no runs in 16 balls, and put on 111 for the ninth wicket with Ken Fiddling.

Consistency then proved elusive. He failed to register a three-figure score in 16 Championship matches in 1948, and although his form improved the following year the competition for batting places, with the arrival of Messrs Oldfield, Livingston and Jakeman, was becoming altogether more robust. He played his last match for Northamptonshire in 1951 and spent the next thirty years working for British Timken, the Northampton-based roller bearings firm with such a distinguished history of supporting sport and sportsmen. Like Dennis Brookes, he celebrated his diamond wedding anniversary in 2000.

Bishan Bedi
RHB and SLA, 1972-77

Born: Amritsar, India, 25 September 1946

Batting Career:

M	I	NO	Runs	HS
110	123	33	1,002	61
53	*34*	*9*	*173*	*24**
Ave	**100**	**50**	**ct/st**	
11.13	-	1	35	
6.92	*-*	*-*	*11*	

Bowling Career:

Runs	Wkts	Ave
9,067	434	20.89
1,486	*53*	*28.04*
BB	**5wi**	**10wm**
7-34	26	5
4-35	*-*	*-*

B ishan Bedi provided a welcome taste of the exotic at Wantage Road in the 1970s. With his brightly-coloured patkas and his complete mastery of flight and spin, the Indian slow left-armer beguiled the eye for half a dozen seasons before his sadly acrimonious departure from the club at the end of 1977.

Bedi constituted one-third of India's potent slow-bowling force which undid England in the deciding Test at The Oval in August 1971. He, Chandrasekhar and Venkataraghavan claimed fifteen wickets between them to set up an historic victory, by which time Northamptonshire had already offered Bedi a three-year contract. Notwithstanding secretary Ken Turner's difficulties with the central heating system in the new Bedi family home in Northampton (he almost managed to burn the house down before his man had even moved in), the signing proved an immediate success.

In 1972, Bedi's first County Ground summer, he captured 75 wickets and played a leading role in Northamptonshire's first-ever win over the Australians. The following year saw him become the first bowler since Haydn Sully in 1966 to take 100 wickets in a season for the club. Batsmen might find themselves being applauded by the Indian magician for a good stroke, but few prospered against him for long. Even when David Hughes 'slogged' (*Wisden*) 26 runs off his final over in the 1976 Gillette Cup final, it somehow seemed like part of Bedi's masterplan for victory. And, of course, Northamptonshire won.

Then, suddenly, it all went sour. As the rest of the cricket world struggled to come to terms with Kerry Packer's coup, Northamptonshire's committee decided in July 1977 to release Bedi at the end of the season. At the same time, stories that the TCCB had concerns over the legitimacy of his bowling action appeared in the newspapers, and the public exchanges between Bedi and the club did nothing to improve the already poisonous atmosphere. His response on the field was to return match figures of 11-107 in a big victory over Middlesex at Wellingborough School.

Bedi subsequently took Northamptonshire to an industrial tribunal for unfair dismissal. The case was heard at Bedford in 1978, and Bedi lost. For a cricketer whose bowling exuded peace and serenity, it was a decidedly stormy parting of the ways.

Ben Bellamy

RHB and WK, 1920-37

Born: Wollaston, Northants, 22 April 1891

Died: Wellingborough, 22 December 1985

Batting Career:

M	I	NO	Runs	HS
353	624	66	9,226	168
Ave	100	50	ct/st	
16.53	4	37	527/125	

Bowling Career:

Runs	Wkts	Ave
57	0	-
BB	5wi	10wm
-	-	-

Ben Bellamy's first-class career with Northamptonshire gave credence to the old adage that everything comes to those who wait. This Wollaston boy joined the County Ground staff in 1912 after impressing coach Charlie Pool, but the First World War and Walter Buswell's cricketing longevity combined to deny him a regular Championship place until 1922, when he was thirty-one. Bellamy then remained the first-choice wicketkeeper for fourteen seasons, and made the last of his 353 appearances – as a batsman, Ken James having taken over the gloves – in 1937.

A tall man for a 'keeper, Bellamy's debut behind the stumps came in one of the most remarkable county matches of all time. Northamptonshire's meeting with Surrey at Northampton in August 1920 produced 1,475 runs – a Championship record for nearly seventy years – and a century in 35 minutes, or thereabouts, for Percy Fender. Bellamy's first victim was Jack Hobbs, and he conceded only 11 byes as the visitors totalled 619-5 declared and 120-2.

When Buswell finally called it a day, at the end of 1921, the succession was wholly straightforward. Bellamy 'took' the new young fast bowler, 'Nobby' Clark, with aplomb, and scored valuable runs too – notably a career-

best 168 against Worcestershire at New Road in 1922. Three years later, he and his Wollaston neighbour, Vernon Murdin, posted 148 for the last wicket against Glamorgan, still a County record going into the 2001 season. He may not have been the most stylish cricketer around, but, then as now, aesthetic considerations counted for nothing in the scorebook. Northamptonshire, usually struggling in this period, were fortunate to have such a sound man in the engine room. Competent cricket was as much a part of his everyday routine as leaving his motorbike at Wellingborough station en route to an away fixture.

He shrugged off a major fitness problem in 1931 when a broken finger became infected, prompting talk of possible amputation, and after his retirement served for twenty-two years as coach at Bedford School. When he died in 1985, aged ninety-four, he was the oldest surviving County Championship cricketer. And, ever the loyal senior pro, in his final months he was still referring to amateurs he had played with six decades before as 'Mister.'

Robin Boyd-Moss

RHB and SLA, 1980-87

Born: Hatton, Ceylon (now Sri Lanka), 16 December 1959

Batting Career:

M	I	NO	Runs	HS
115	190	18	5,044	155
68	*64*	*9*	*1,394*	*99*
Ave	**100**	**50**	**ct/st**	
29.32	8	31	48	
25.35	*-*	*7*	*18*	

Bowling Career:

Runs	Wkts	Ave		
1,294	25	51.76		
84	*3*	*28.00*		
BB	**5wi**	**10wm**		
3-39	-	-		
3-47	*-*	*-*		

On a sunny August morning in 1982, two Northamptonshire batsmen smashed Derbyshire's attack – and their front-line bowlers, mark you – to the tune of 182 runs in 98 minutes, hastening a declaration which led, ultimately, to an emphatic victory. At one end was India's Kapil Dev, already established as one of the leading all-rounders in Test cricket; at the other, a Cambridge University student named Robin Boyd-Moss, who followed his 137 in the first innings with an unbeaten 80 and matched his illustrious colleague shot for shot.

Boyd-Moss, then twenty-two, ended the season with 1,602 first-class runs at 44.50, and earned the County some new video equipment as the Commercial Union Young Batsman of the Year. In 1983 he gained the last of his four blues, and became the first player in the 156-year history of the fixture to score two hundreds in the same Varsity match. For good measure, he claimed 5-27 with his left-arm spin in Oxford's second knock. Almost inevitably in view of his background, the former Bedford School pupil was already being talked of as a future Northamptonshire captain. It was only, surely, a matter of time. And yet, within five years his cricket career was over. Shortly before the start of the 1988 season he surprised more or less everyone by announcing his retirement, opting to settle in Kenya and run a garage business.

In truth, Boyd-Moss's self-confidence, never particularly robust, had been battered by a series of untimely setbacks. In 1984, his first full summer with the County, he suffered a broken thumb when playing well, and then contracted hepatitis; a year later, back trouble kept him out of action until mid-June; centuries against Lancashire and Glamorgan set him up for a successful season in 1986, only for form to desert him in the closing weeks; then fitness problems allowed him only half a dozen matches in 1987, triggering the decision to move his life in a different direction.

Boyd-Moss's premature departure from the scene would have been much less of a disappointment to County supporters, had he not offered tantalising glimpses of a very considerable talent.

Vince Broderick

LHB and SLA, 1939-57

Born: Bacup, Lancashire 17 August 1920

Batting Career:

M	I	NO	Runs	HS
245	373	42	7,224	190
Ave	**100**	**50**	**ct/st**	
21.88	6	30	64	

Bowling Career:

Runs	Wkts	Ave
14,338	530	27.05
BB	**5wi**	**10wm**
9-35	22	4

For a couple of seasons just after the Second World War, the England selectors were keeping an eye on Vince Broderick, Northamptonshire's left-arm-spinning all-rounder. The tall, gently humorous Lancastrian was chosen for the 1948 Test trial at Edgbaston, and accounted for Jack Robertson, Joe Hardstaff and Godfrey Evans before the rain came. They had another look at him in the corresponding match a year later, and again he performed creditably. But the call to higher things never came.

Broderick was taken on Northamptonshire's groundstaff at £3 a week in 1939, and made his County debut against Glamorgan at Cardiff a few days before Hitler invaded Poland. He became a first team regular in 1947, and although not a big spinner of the ball, relying more on flight and 'dip', he claimed 75 Championship wickets that year, including 8-16 when Derbyshire visited Rushden. Many thought he stood a realistic chance of making the MCC's winter tour to the West Indies, but Yorkshire's Johnny Wardle got the nod instead.

In 1948 he performed the 'double' in all first-class cricket, and destroyed Sussex with 9-35 on a drying pitch at Horsham. To set the seal on his memorable summer, 'Brod' also registered his first two centuries, against Warwickshire and Essex. Frustratingly, when one more solid push might well have forced open the international door, he took a step or two backwards in 1949. Indeed, it may reasonably be said that his career had already peaked, as batsmen around the circuit fathomed his bowling out. However, he remained a hard-working member of the side until his retirement in 1957, and then took charge of Northamptonshire's Second XI before heading south to begin a long and successful stint as professional at Winchester School. He stayed for twenty-eight years, only hanging up his boots in 1987.

Broderick's prowess as an opening batsman kept his name in Northamptonshire's record books for more than four decades. He and 'Buddy' Oldfield put on 361 for the first wicket against Scotland in 1953 – a figure only surpassed in 1996, by Mal Loye and Richard Montgomerie against Yorkshire. Broderick looked set for a first-class double century, but faltered just ten runs short.

Dennis Brookes

RHB, 1934-59

Born: Kippax, Yorks, 29 October 1915
Batting Career:

M	I	NO	Runs	HS
492	871	69	28,980	257
Ave	**100**	**50**	**ct/st**	
36.13	67	141	192	

Bowling Career:

Runs	Wkts	Ave
127	3	42.33
BB	**5wi**	**10wm**
1-7	-	-

The old distinctions between the gentleman and the player were never less clearly defined, surely, than in the case of Dennis Brookes. A professional immensely proud of his cricketing craftsmanship, he has served the wider community of Northampton – as a Justice of the Peace for twenty-six years, five of them as Chairman of the Bench – with the same diligence as he showed in opening the innings for Northamptonshire during a career spanning a quarter of a century. In 1982 he became the first former pro. to be elected the club's president, and in the summer of 2000 – some sixty-eight years after his first visit to Wantage Road as a trialist – was still absorbing every nuance of each day's play at the County Ground, where the main gates now bear his name.

It was, in fact, the typing that clinched it. The committee minutes for 1933 record that the teenager was 'to be offered terms, a clerkship and lodgings to be found, and so much pocket money paid.' Brookes recalls that secretary Eric Coley was keen to discover if he could use a typewriter, and so be in a position to help out in the office: 'I don't think I would have been taken on otherwise!' Nearly 30,000 first-class runs and 67 centuries later, the penny dropped that he could handle a bat as well.

With no Second XI cricket in which to hone his skills, the young man from Kippax turned out in semi-social matches for the Club and Ground side and Northants Amateurs. It was not the ideal preparation for a Championship debut against his native Yorkshire at Bradford in 1934. Hedley Verity trapped him leg-before for a single in the first innings – 'playing back when I should have been forward' – but a few kindly words of encouragement from the great Herbert Sutcliffe offered hope for the future. He scored his maiden century against the New Zealanders in 1937, an innings which helped him past 1,000 runs for the first time; it was a feat he would repeat in each of the next sixteen seasons, exceeding 2,000 in 1946, 1949 and 1952.

'Upright in his stance, calm in his demeanour, he scorned violent movements of the bat, gleaning runs almost imperceptibly with silky drives, subtle deflections and intuitive running between the wickets.' So wrote Frank Tyson of Brookes, who was already nearing forty when 'Typhoon' blew into town. R.C. Robertson-

Dennis and Freda Brookes at the official opening of the gates bearing his name, in 1997.

Glasgow, assessing him as a younger player, reckoned that 'Dennis Brookes has the look of an England batsman, not merely of a man who happens, by a set of curious chances, to play for a team called England.' Most judges have been particularly generous in their praise of his skill against spin. It is no surprise that he himself rates not one of his 6 double-centuries – not even the record-equalling 257 at Bristol in 1949 – as the best innings of his career, but 105 out of 185 against Kent's Doug Wright on a turning pitch at Northampton in 1952.

He made a solitary Test appearance against the West Indies in Barbados on 'Gubby' Allen's 1947/48 expedition. In 1946, umpire Frank Chester told him – after he had done twelfth man duty for England in the first two of the summer's Tests against India – that if they picked him for the Players against the Gentlemen, he would be certain to go to Australia with Wally Hammond. They didn't, and despite being measured for his MCC blazer

by the man from Simpson's – at Hammond's insistence – his name wasn't on the final list. Freddie Brown sounded him out about going to India as senior professional on the 1951/52 trip, but again nothing came of it.

Brookes captained Northamptonshire from 1954 to 1957, and in his last year in charge the side finished as runners-up to Surrey in the Championship. He was promptly eased out of the job in favour of Raman Subba Row, but played on loyally until retiring from the first-class game in 1959. Thereafter he led the Second XI until 1968, coached, worked in the office as Ken Turner's assistant-secretary and served on the committee before being honoured with the presidency.

He celebrated both his diamond wedding anniversary – having married Freda in March 1940 – and his eighty-fifth birthday in 2000, and still takes a daily walk (summer or winter) around the County Ground's perimeter. No one has graced the old place for so long, with such distinction, in so many different capacities.

27

Freddie Brown
RHB and RM or LB, 1949-53

Born: Lima, Peru, 16 December 1910
Died: Ramsbury, Wilts, 24 July 1991
Batting Career:

M	I	NO	Runs	HS
102	153	13	4,331	171*
Ave	100	50	ct/st	
30.93	7	22	69	

Bowling Career:

Runs	Wkts	Ave
9,083	391	23.23
BB	5wi	10wm
7-33	17	4

Northamptonshire's energetic recruiting drive in the immediate post-war period produced batsmen (Oldfield and Barron), bowlers (Nutter and Gordon Garlick) and a wicketkeeper (Ken Fiddling). What it didn't throw up, with no disrespect to Arthur Childs-Clarke, the London club cricketer who skippered in 1947 and 1948, was a credible leader. Until, of course, Freddie Brown came along. He shouldered the task, begun by Robert Nelson, of restoring the county club's self-esteem, and achieved it in the course of five seasons during which dull moments were few and far between.

Brown's reputation as an all-rounder was forged in the 1930s with Cambridge University and Surrey. He earned an England debut in 1931, aged twenty, and was the 'baby' on the infamous 1932/33 tour to Australia under Douglas Jardine, although not selected for any of the Tests until reaching New Zealand. Taken prisoner at Tobruk in June 1942, he lost nearly five stone during his three years 'in the bag', and had drifted out of the regular first-class game by the time Northamptonshire expressed an interest.

They tentatively tapped him up in 1947, only to be rebuffed with a fairly curt 'not interested.' But they tried again a year later, with the backing of the estimable John Pascoe at British Timken who guaranteed him a winter job with 'reasonable prospects' for his post-cricket future. Brown decided to give it a go.

His first selection meeting, before the visit to Taunton in May 1949, has passed into Northamptonshire folklore. Rawlins Hawtin's committee was busy discussing who might or might not be available when Brown interrupted proceedings, pulled out a piece of paper and said: 'I'm sorry. But I'm the only one, with Jack Mercer and Dennis Brookes, who has been at all the net practices and this is the team I want.' Or words to that effect. Brown got his way, guided his chosen men to a tense victory over Somerset by two wickets, and the die was cast. By the end of that season Northamptonshire had climbed from bottom to sixth place in the Championship, while Brown had done the 'double' in all matches and led England in the last two Tests of the summer against Walter Hadlee's Kiwis. The lights even came back on in Northampton town centre after the years of war and austerity. It was a startling transformation all round.

Freddie Brown's breezy approach brought him friends and admirers all over the cricket world – not least in Australia.

The County never finished as high again during his reign, a fact attributable in part to his absences on international duty – first as captain, then as a selector. Vince Broderick has maintained that Brown's runs and wickets were more important to Northamptonshire than his leadership; Brian Reynolds, quick to praise his old skipper as a man who never asked you to do something he wouldn't do himself, was also full of admiration for his stamina.

One day at Neath, the forty-two-year-old – and heavily perspiring – Brown sent down 49 overs in Glamorgan's innings, claiming 5-83: 'He bowled inners, outers, offers and finally leggers,' recalls Reynolds. A large gin and tonic (rather than isotonic) at lunchtime set him up for the rigours of the afternoon session. He could also be destructive with the bat, smashing 101 – including 20 off a Ray Dovey over – in his final home match for the County, against Kent at Wantage Road in 1953.

Brown earned the respect of all Australia with his lion-hearted efforts as England's captain in the 1950/51 series, and kept the job against South Africa the following summer. A member of the Northamptonshire committee once asked him who he put first, county or country. 'England – and if you did too, we might get on a bit better,' was the reply. He later compounded the felony in his autobiography *Cricket Musketeer* by making the not unreasonable observation that a club committee comprising thirty-nine members might be a touch unwieldy. Brown was not a man to hide his feelings, as slack fielders soon discovered.

In a 'poacher-turned-gamekeeper' scenario he spent more than twenty years on the committee himself, and was an officer emeritus from 1975 until his death. He worked tirelessly for other cricketing organisations, particularly the National Cricket Association, and served as president of MCC in 1971/72. Dennis Silk, who gave the address at Freddie Brown's funeral in 1991, encapsulated his old friend's qualities perfectly when he stated that: 'He was a giant in spirit as well as in stature.'

William 'Beau' Brown

RHB, 1925-37

Born: Wellingborough, 13 November 1900
Died: Hove, Sussex, 20 January 1986
Batting Career:

M	I	NO	Runs	HS
127	214	29	2,601	103*
Ave	**100**	**50**	**ct/st**	
14.05	1	2	57	

Bowling Career:

Runs	Wkts	Ave
1	0	-
BB	**5wi**	**10wm**
-	-	-

When, in his later years, 'Beau' Brown became secretary of a local branch of the RSPCA in Sussex, the cynics were heard to mutter that his long involvement with Northamptonshire County Cricket Club would have prepared him well for the post. Although not a great player, this popular solicitor was a loyal servant to the club in various roles at a time when it needed each and every ounce of goodwill.

He never threatened to secure a place in the Cambridge University XI of the early 1920s, but turned out enthusiastically for Northants Amateurs and other local clubs, and was drafted in to make his Northamptonshire debut against Dublin University – including future Nobel Prize winner Samuel Beckett, whose stay in the second innings was cut short by Brown's catch – at the County Ground in 1925. Three years later, he scored his only first-class century in 214 visits to the crease, taking an unbeaten 103 off Glamorgan.

In autumn 1931, following a crisis meeting of members at which Northamptonshire's possible withdrawal from the County Championship was seriously discussed, Vallance Jupp resigned the captaincy and Brown – after initially declining the committee's invitation on health grounds – replaced him. The new skipper, an altogether more diplomatic individual than his predecessor, immediately paved the way for the return of fast bowler 'Nobby' Clark, who had fallen out with Jupp in a big way. Brown led his men to a fine innings victory over the 1933 West Indians and stayed in charge until an injury sustained when he trod on a ball forced him to hand over the reins in 1935.

But his devotion to the cause remained undimmed, and upon Eric Coley's resignation as secretary in the winter of 1937/38 Brown volunteered to do the job on an honorary basis. He kept the minutes up to 1942 and later became Northamptonshire's official statistician. His final act on the club's behalf, on the day he went into hospital for the last time, was to inform *Wisden* of the death of his old team-mate, Ben Bellamy.

Cheerfully aware of his limitations on the field of play, he gave freely of his time and energy through some of the club's very darkest days before and during the Second World War.

Born: Welford, Northants, 12 January 1875			
Died: Swinford, Leics, 24 April 1950				
Batting Career:				
M	**I**	**NO**	**Runs**	**HS**
205	327	76	2,670	101*
Ave	**100**	**50**	**ct/st**	
10.63	1	2	283/115	

Bowling Career:		
Runs	**Wkts**	**Ave**
-	-	-
-	-	-
BB	**5wi**	**10wm**
-	-	-
-	-	-

The son of a Leicestershire county cricketer, Walter Buswell was born in the village of Welford, just the right side of Northamptonshire's border with 'the old enemy.' In common with both his immediate predecessor and immediate successor as the County's first-choice wicketkeeper, Charlie Smith and Ben Bellamy, he played on well into middle age, making the last of his 205 appearances as a forty-six-year-old in 1921.

Sound rather than greatly gifted behind the stumps – 'I went there first because nobody else would go' he admitted years later – the solidly-built Buswell usually chose to stand back to his great friend, George Thompson. The pair spent countless hours yarning, both during and after their playing careers, and when Buswell joined the first-class umpires list (he served from 1923 to 1937) he often stayed with Thompson on his trips to Bristol.

Perhaps they reminisced from time to time about their visit to the House of Commons in 1909 as guests of some of the county's Members of Parliament. Buswell, a farmer outside cricket, seized the opportunity to make known his strong views on the new Small Holdings Act. It is not recorded whether the honourable gentlemen were impressed by his arguments, but Thompson certainly wasn't; 'all rot' was his damning verdict.

Although Buswell had been groomed as the heir to the seemingly indestructible Smith, who eventually retired in 1906, he was not without competition. Harold Ellis from Burnley and 'Tim' Manning, captain from 1908 to 1910, both took the gloves from him on occasions, and it was only in 1911 that Buswell could really call the job his own. He was an ever-present in the memorable Championship campaign of 1912, and although not the most cultured of batsmen he did manage a somewhat surprising first-class century, against Warwickshire in 1914.

Buswell claimed nearly 400 dismissals for Northamptonshire, and was happily able to play alongside Thompson for one last season when the great all-rounder returned in 1921 after his serious wartime illness. Always a trier to the last ounce on the field, he continued to follow the County's fortunes as a spectator right up to his death.

David Capel
RHB and RFM, 1981-98

Born: Northampton, 6 February 1963
Batting Career:

M	I	NO	Runs	HS
270	407	56	10,869	175
296	*266*	*46*	*6,177*	*121*
Ave	**100**	**50**	**ct/st**	
30.96	15	64	134	
28.08	*4*	*25*	*74*	

Bowling Career:

Runs	Wkts	Ave
14,780	467	31.65
7,498	*236*	*31.77*
BB	**5wi**	**10wm**
7-44	13	-
5-51	*1*	-

To see David Capel in charge of the Northamptonshire Young Cricketers Under-19s squad on their tour to South Africa in April 2000 was to gain a pretty good idea of what makes him tick. Having made the journey himself from the County Colts to an England cap, leaving no stone unturned in his quest for maximum effectiveness, both technical and mental, he puts himself about to a comparable degree on behalf of his young charges – provided they are willing to at least match his commitment. The club's cricket academy, now up and running, offers Northamptonshire's Director of Excellence a fresh and exciting challenge.

A Northamptonian to the sprigs in the boots he used to make as a teenager, Capel gave up producing cricket footwear for the likes of Mike Hendrick and Graham Dilley to join the Wantage Road staff in 1980. His first-class debut came against the Sri Lankans the following year, and in 1982 he opened his account of Championship wickets by dismissing Geoffrey Boycott cheaply at Middlesbrough. He began to attract interest from further afield in 1986, the summer that

saw him awarded his County cap, culminating in a trip to Sharjah with an England squad captained by John Emburey. He returned home in April 1987 to embark on a memorable season.

The highlights tumbled over each other; two Lord's finals with Northamptonshire, driving handsomely on his way to 97 off 110 balls in the Benson & Hedges Cup decider against Yorkshire; a memorable all-round performance (7-46 followed by a decisive 91 not out) to defeat the same opponents in the Championship and celebrate his call-up for the Third Test against Pakistan; and then that debut at Headingley as the first Northampton-born Test cricketer since George Thompson in 1910. It was *Wilson of the Wizard* material. England were floundering at 30-5 when Capel came to the crease and made 53 in three-and-a-quarter hours, comfortably the top-scorer in an otherwise execrable batting display.

This was the first of his 15 appearances, and he rarely let England down. In Karachi four months later, on Mike Gatting's ill-tempered expedition to Pakistan, Capel battled his way to 98 before Abdul Qadir's googly denied him a century. Against the West Indies at Port-of-Spain in 1990 his knock of 40 – 'an innings of considerable courage at a vulnerable time'

One of Northamptonshire's fiercest competitors over the years, David Capel always showed great determination with bat or ball.

according to *Wisden* – should have paved the way for victory, but for a combination of poor light and the home side's appalling over-rate. In the next Test, in Barbados, he sent back Viv Richards twice, but wasn't selected again after that series.

For Northamptonshire, 'Capes' never lost his competitive edge. He enjoyed an outstanding summer in 1989, logging 1,290 runs and 55 wickets to secure his trip to the Caribbean, and after a couple of injury-ravaged years bounced back to do his bit in the County's quest for honours in 1995. Always one to relish a good, old-fashioned, eyeball to eyeball cricketing scrap, he was seen to excellent advantage in the epic Championship contest with Warwickshire at Edgbaston, described afterwards by both captains – Allan Lamb and Dermot Reeve – as the best four-day match they had experienced.

Capel's contribution was 50 out of 152 all out in the first innings, then a career-best 7-44 in Warwickshire's reply, and finally the wicket of Tim Munton to seal a magnificent seven-run triumph.

Although he objected strongly to the gimmicky term 'pinch-hitter', Capel filled the 'attacking opener' role with some success in the 1996 Benson & Hedges Cup competition, helping Northamptonshire to the final. Had he been used more sparingly as a bowler down the seasons, his stay in first-class cricket might have been longer; as it was, the end came midway through 1998 at the age of thirty-five. The club paid tribute to his 'passion and emotion' on the field – two key words, those, in the Capel make-up – and handed him the responsibility, shouldered with characteristic pride, of nurturing the Northamptonshire players of tomorrow.

Bob Carter
RHB and RM, 1978-82

Born: King's Lynn, Norfolk, 25 May 1960				
Batting Career:				
M	**I**	**NO**	**Runs**	**HS**
51	67	15	858	79
48	*27*	*12*	*152*	*21**
Ave	**100**	**50**	**ct/st**	
16.50	-	1	29	
10.13	*-*	*-*	*17*	
Bowling Career:				
Runs	**Wkts**	**Ave**		
1,492	38	39.26		
712	*27*	*26.37*		
BB	**5wi**	**10wm**		
4-27	-	-		
3-35	*-*	*-*		

Northamptonshire County Cricket Club has apparently exerted a magnetic pull on Bob Carter for the last quarter of a century. When he returned to Wantage Road as Director of Cricket in 1999 it marked the beginning of his third 'career' with the club, following spells as player and coach. His knowledge of, and feeling for, Northamptonshire, coupled with a rigorous attention to detail, convinced the committee that he was the right man to engineer a revival after several disappointing seasons, and that view was borne out by the events of 2000 when Carter and Matthew Hayden masterminded the successful County Championship and National League campaigns.

'Cooch' Carter joined Northamptonshire in 1976 as a seventeen-year-old all-rounder from King's Lynn, and made his debut in 1978 – a year that ended with his selection for the Young England tour to Australia, managed by Freddie Brown and Keith Andrew. He performed usefully in three-day and limited-overs cricket over five seasons – notching a few runs here, picking up a handy wicket

there, and always outstanding in the field – but did not do enough to earn a new contract at the end of 1982.

He headed for New Zealand, played some first-class cricket for Canterbury, and early in 1985 was on his way back to Wantage Road as assistant-coach, running the Second XI and Colts team. When Brian Reynolds became Northamptonshire's first Cricket Development Officer a year later, Carter succeeded him as head coach, remaining in that job until 1995 and forging an effective partnership with the captain, Allan Lamb.

His frustration at the club's unwillingness to offer him the responsibility and long-term security he desired saw him fly back to New Zealand to take up a post running Wellington cricket, but he never lost touch with Northamptonshire and watched from a distance as the appointment of John Emburey in 1996 failed to produce the hoped-for results. So, in the autumn of 1998, supporters learned of Carter's third coming. Stressing the importance of a long-term development agenda, he actively encouraged the establishment of a Northamptonshire cricket academy, which admitted its first intake of seven young cricketers in November 2000.

Born: Elton, Hunts, 9 August 1902
Died: King's Lynn, Norfolk, 28 April 1982
Batting Career:

M	I	NO	Runs	HS
307	447	176	1,809	30
Ave	**100**	**50**	**ct/st**	
6.67	-	-	101	

Bowling Career:

Runs	Wkts	Ave
23,387	1,097	21.31
BB	**5wi**	**10wm**
8-59	59	14

Edward Winchester Clark – 'Nobby' as a matter of course – took more first-class wickets for Northamptonshire than any other cricketer before or since. How many more he would have claimed, but for a relationship with the club which for most of the 1930s alternated between armed truce and open warfare, can only be a matter for conjecture.

Possessing a left-arm fast bowler's action so aesthetically pleasing that it was used in an advertising poster for Worthington beer, Clark's temperament 'veered like a cardboard weathercock' according to R.C. Robertson-Glasgow. 'Plum' Warner reckoned that six months with the Royal Marines wouldn't have done him any harm, 'for at Deal they tame tigers.' But when he stood at the end of his run picking the mud out of his spikes – a sure sign, said team-mates, that he was interested in proceedings – the batsman knew a severe test awaited.

Born just the other side of Northamptonshire's border with Huntingdonshire, Clark came to Wantage Road by an unexpectedly circuitous route. Apprenticed to an engineering firm in Bradford, he had an outstanding 1921 season in league cricket up there, prompting Frank Field, the former Warwickshire player, to recommend him to Northamptonshire. He topped the

County's bowling averages in 1922 with 20 wickets at 17.10, and 'did so well in a few matches as to inspire some hope for the future' in the opinion of *Wisden*.

He reached 100 wickets for the first time in 1926, appeared in two Test Trials the following year, and got the nod from the selectors for the final game against the 1929 South Africans at The Oval. It was a fitting climax to the best summer of his career – 141 wickets for Northamptonshire at less than 19 runs apiece – but also presaged the first of his major disputes with officialdom.

In July 1930 Clark asked the committee for permission to fit in a Saturday game for Rochdale, and duly received it; the County had no fixture that day, and it would earn the bowler an extra £20. But the captain, Vallance Jupp, then reported Clark for 'insubordination' during a match at Worcester, and permission to go north was withdrawn. He went anyway, and the committee sacked him. He subsequently played league cricket for Todmorden, and made far more money than Northamptonshire could have afforded at the time.

A bowling action worth advertising; 'Nobby' Clark at his peak in the 1930s.

In 1932, with Jupp – not one of nature's conciliators – out of the captaincy, Clark returned and fitted in as many county matches as his commitments with Todmorden allowed. His Test career resumed in 1933, after a ten-wicket haul helped Northamptonshire inflict an innings defeat on the touring West Indians, and the next summer he became the first County player since George Thompson in 1909 to represent England against Australia. He accounted for five illustrious names – Brown, Ponsford, McCabe, Kippax and Chipperfield – in the second innings of the Oval Test, and also beat Bradman all ends up, 'only to miss the wicket by the narrowest possible margin' reported Douglas Jardine, Clark's captain on the previous winter's MCC trip to India, from the press box.

Northamptonshire remained wary of him. He would not tug his forelock when the great and good entered the dressing room, and on at least one occasion caused a certain amount of spluttering by informing a prominent committee member, E.E. Caesar, that it was 'a thousand pounds to a pinch of shit' that the County would lose the upcoming match. Reliable slip-fielders were at a premium, and the references to Madame Tussauds as another chance went begging became more frequent. Against Middlesex at Lord's in 1936 he was magnificent, bagging 12-131 in the game; within a year he been sacked again, in the wake of complaints from skipper Geoffrey Cuthbertson.

As a coda to his tempestuous career, Clark agreed match terms to help Northamptonshire out in 1946. Even at the age of forty-three he was sharp enough for a few overs with the new ball to offer a glimpse or two of the pre-war Test bowler. He played his last game for the County in 1947, not one whit less aggressive than when he replaced 'Bumper' Wells a quarter of a century before.

Bowling he liked, batting he did not. He accepted it, in Robertson-Glasgow's words, as 'a professional duty', while fielding was 'an undignified interval between two overs.'

Bob Clarke
LHB and LFM, 1947-57

Born: Finedon, Northants, 22 April 1924
Died: Sherborne, Dorset, 3 August 1981

Batting Career:

M	I	NO	Runs	HS
208	257	83	2,664	56
Ave	**100**	**50**	**ct/st**	
15.31	-	5	146	

Bowling Career:

Runs	Wkts	Ave
16,397	477	34.37
BB	**5wi**	**10wm**
8-26	16	1

According to Frank Tyson, one of his new-ball partners for Northamptonshire in the 1950s, Bob Clarke 'was living evidence that the early Viking invaders once sailed up the Nene valley as far as Finedon. Flaxen-haired, barrel-chested and built like a bull, he could have been the reincarnation of a Norseman.'

He ravaged county batting line-ups, notably in 1949 and 1953, and was hailed as a worthy successor to another left-arm paceman, 'Nobby' Clark, who had just retired. But he failed to realise his early potential, and dropped out of the first-class game in 1957.

Clarke served in the Royal Navy for six years, spending the war on the cruiser HMS *Glasgow* in various theatres from the Arctic to the Bay of Biscay and most points in-between, and made his Northamptonshire debut in 1947. He was not afraid of hard work, sending down 843 overs in 1949 – more, even, than the new captain, Freddie Brown – for 88 wickets. His value to the side was augmented by his skill as a close catcher, while his batting down the order reflected his general approach to the game: wholehearted and uncomplicated.

On his day, with the ball swinging, Clarke could be as destructive a bowler as any in the country. He claimed 13-190 in the game against Surrey at Northampton in 1949, wrecked Hampshire with 8-26 at Peterborough two years later, and in 1953, statistically his best season, he finished with 97 wickets at 24.74. After that, injury reduced his effectiveness and ended his career at thirty-three.

An endearing character, Bob Clarke's exploits on and off the field have been immortalised in some of the County Ground's most enduring stories, not all apocryphal. He may have tried the patience of his skipper now and then, but when it all came good even the no-nonsense Brown – whose autobiography contains the deathless line 'Bob Clarke has not got a very acute cricket brain' – was willing to forgive him the occasional trespass. Perhaps when you have sailed with convoys to Murmansk, with disaster and sudden death close at your elbow, even a verbal rocket from F.R. Brown becomes an altogether less intimidating prospect.

Geoff Cook

RHB, 1971-90

Born: Middlesbrough, 9 October 1951				
Batting Career:				
M	**I**	**NO**	**Runs**	**HS**
415	711	62	20,976	203
358	*334*	*28*	*8,218*	*130*
Ave	**100**	**50**	**ct/st**	
32.32	33	101	380/3	
26.86	*4*	*33*	*140*	

Bowling Career:		
Runs	**Wkts**	**Ave**
548	3	182.66
10	*0*	*-*
BB	**5wi**	**10wm**
1-7	-	-
-	-	-

Geoff Cook's reign as captain of Northamptonshire is, to date, the longest since the County achieved first-class status. Given a modicum of good fortune and, with the benefit of hindsight, a different tactical decision here and there, he would have lifted two or three trophies on the club's behalf. As it is, leaving aside all the wrung-dry arguments about 'The Under-achieving Eighties', Cook will be remembered as a cricketer who gave everything for the cause, regardless of personal discomfort; who scored more than 20,000 runs, many of them when they were needed most; who put plenty back into the game, as chairman of the Cricketers' Association; and who, from a journalist's point of view, always responded to a sensible question with a sensible answer.

After coming down as trialist from Middlesbrough in 1968 he made his debut against Leicestershire three years later, and was soon promoted from the middle-order to open the innings. His early progress was not spectacular, but he achieved a breakthrough in 1975 when he passed 1,000 runs for the first time. In any case, his skill as a close-catcher, fearless at forward short leg despite some nasty knocks, made him pretty much an automatic selection. There was also his thoughtful and intelligent approach to cricket which, from an early stage, marked him out as a potential skipper. He was appointed vice-captain to Jim Watts in 1978, following the departure of several senior players, and with Watts managing only a dozen Championship games that summer after the death of his wife, Cook had plenty of opportunity to develop his leadership skills.

Also in 1978, he formed an opening partnership with Wayne Larkins which was to flourish for more than a decade. They became 'The Old Firm' and complemented each other perfectly – Cook sound and solid, Larkins bold and brilliant. Occasionally, just occasionally, the roles were reversed. 'Harry' and 'Ned' became such an item at Wantage Road, linked inextricably in the minds of all Northamptonshire followers, that their subsequent fall-out over Larkins' sacking from Durham in 1995 shocked and saddened many at their old club.

Cook came within a foot or so of securing some silverware in his first official season as captain in 1981, following Watts' retirement. He hit 111 from 148 balls in the NatWest Trophy final against Derbyshire, falling to a

Geoff Cook's value to Northamptonshire as player and captain was immense, although trophies eluded him.

leg-before decision that still causes head-shaking in the West Stand today, and then saw Geoff Miller and Colin Tunnicliffe scramble a leg-bye off the last ball to tie the scores and take the cup by virtue of losing fewer wickets. The game was to have momentous consequences. Cook, Man of the Match in a losing cause, earned a place on that winter's England tour to India and Sri Lanka. Larkins didn't, and opted to join the 'rebel' expedition to South Africa. Cook made the first of his 7 Test appearances in Colombo, the last in Sydney a year later; two half-centuries in the home series against India in 1982 failed to secure him a long-term international future.

That Northamptonshire were a side worth watching in the mid-1980s was due in no small measure to Cook's enterprising approach as a Championship skipper. Declarations were made, challenges accepted, and results overall were better than a team with limited bowling resources might reasonably have expected. A different scenario may have unfolded had the club's attempts to sign Courtney Walsh in 1984 come to fruition. He then took the County to Lord's twice in 1987, losing in another 'tie' to Yorkshire in the Benson & Hedges Cup, and to Richard Hadlee-inspired Nottinghamshire in a NatWest decider which descended into farce as catch after catch went down. It was a heartbreaking 'double' for all concerned, and Cook felt the disappointment more keenly than anyone.

He stayed on as captain in 1988, only to resign at the end of the season in the hope that someone with 'fresh ideas and fresh motivation' would be able to take the team forward. After an uneasy couple of years in the ranks he headed north again to assume a central role in overseeing Durham's promotion into English cricket's top flight.

Nick Cook

RHB and SLA, 1986-94

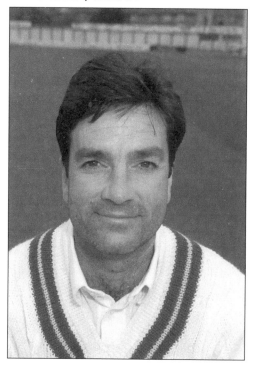

Born: Leicester, 17 June 1956

Batting Career:

M	I	NO	Runs	HS
167	171	39	1,487	64
165	*68*	*29*	*375*	*21**
Ave	**100**	**50**	**ct/st**	
11.26	-	2	93	
9.62	*-*	*-*	*52*	

Bowling Career:

Runs	Wkts	Ave
10,425	371	28.09
5,087	*153*	*33.25*
BB	**5wi**	**10wm**
7-34	11	1
4-22	*-*	*-*

A shrewd, sociable and articulate cricketer, rarely lacking an opinion on anything from the state of English spin bowling to the runners and riders at Towcester racecourse, via Leicester City's most recent home fixture, Nick Cook finished his first-class career with a creditable haul of 879 wickets at 29 runs apiece. He then turned his attentions to developing the cricketers of tomorrow, and became Northamptonshire's Second XI coach in 1996.

Cook left his native Leicestershire at the end of 1985, complaining of feeling 'unwanted' and frustrated at the seamer-friendly nature of the pitches at Grace Road. His move down the A50 to Northampton enabled him to form a spin partnership with Roger Harper, and in 1986 Cook captured 64 wickets in 870 overs, including a match-winning 5-14 as Essex, the eventual County Champions, were dismissed for only 44 at Colchester. He rounded off the decade successfully with 66 wickets in 1988, and another 56 at only 18.67 to head the Northamptonshire averages the following year.

His impressive form in 1989 earned him a recall to the England side. He appeared in three of the six Tests against Australia, bringing to a close an international career which had begun in such spectacular fashion with 17 wickets in two games, at Lord's and Trent Bridge, against the 1983 New Zealanders. His book about England's Test fortunes in the 1980s, written in collaboration with journalist Neville Scott, was subtitled *The Years of Indecision*, and Cook had more reason than most to appreciate its aptness; dropped in 1984, recalled for the tour to Pakistan in 1987/88, then dropped again until England found themselves under the cosh against Allan Border's men in 1989. The caprices of the selectors were all the more baffling because the country was not exactly overflowing with talented slow left-armers in that period.

Nick Cook had his supporters when Northamptonshire were considering a successor to his namesake, Geoff, as captain. Allan Lamb was appointed instead, and Cook subsequently struggled for fitness and confidence, dropping out of first team cricket in 1994. In his new role, he guided his young charges to the 'double' of Second XI Championship and Aon Risk Trophy in 1998.

Bob Cottam

RHB and RFM, 1972-76

Born: Cleethorpes, Lincs, 16 October 1944

Batting Career:

M	I	NO	Runs	HS
76	86	23	590	62*
68	*42*	*13*	*188*	*23**
Ave	**100**	**50**	**ct/st**	
9.36	-	1	60	
6.48	*-*	*-*	*21*	

Bowling Career:

Runs	Wkts	Ave
4,877	241	20.23
2,066	*87*	*23.75*
BB	**5wi**	**10wm**
8-14	17	2
4-17	*-*	*-*

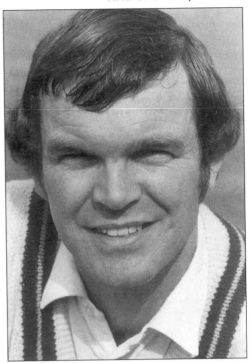

The entirely necessary team rebuilding programme in the early 1970s brought fast bowler Bob Cottam to Northamptonshire from Hampshire, and he had three productive summers with his new county before injury reduced his effectiveness and prompted an early retirement from the first-class game in 1976. Acknowledging the considerable impact he had on the team's fortunes, the Annual Report for that year commented: 'His service to the club, although short in time, was a valuable one.'

Cottam's efforts with Hampshire – including 9-25 against Lancashire in 1965, still a county record – earned him an England call-up for the 1968/69 tour to Pakistan, but by the end of 1971 he had his heart set on a move. He joined Northamptonshire at the same time as John Dye and Bishan Bedi, and although prevented by the registration regulations from playing competitive cricket until mid-June 1972, he demonstrated his appetite for wickets with 8-14 against Oxford University in The Parks, claiming his first five victims for Northamptonshire at a cost of only three runs.

Then, getting down to business in earnest, Cottam picked up 41 Championship wickets in what was left of the season, and the selectors recalled him to the international scene for Tony Lewis's trip to the subcontinent. Everything continued to go to plan on his return; 69 wickets for the County in 1973, another 56 in 1974, and all the time Northamptonshire warranting the status of serious Championship contenders under the captaincy of Jim Watts. Less of a 'tearaway' bowler by this stage, he undid good batsmen with seam and cut while still possessing the ability to fly one around the ears. Unfortunately, a foot problem troubled him during 1975, and although he began the following year back at his best with a match-winning 7-39 at Old Trafford in April, he failed to see out the season and was released at his own request.

Cottam went to coach at a school in Lyme Regis, and graduated to become the National Cricket Association's chief coach in the West Country. After stints with Warwickshire (1988-90) and Somerset (1992-96) he took on the role of specialist bowling coach within the England set-up.

Arthur Cox
RHB and LB, 1926-47

Born: Northampton, 22 July 1907
Died: Northampton, 13 November 1986

Batting Career:

M	I	NO	Runs	HS
229	409	31	6,623	104
Ave	100	50	ct/st	
17.52	1	31	121	

Bowling Career:

Runs	Wkts	Ave
7,926	199	39.82
BB	5wi	10wm
7-91	4	-

Cricket, and specifically Northamptonshire cricket, ran through Arthur Cox's family like a maroon thread. His father, Mark, a left-handed all-rounder, played for the County between 1897 and 1919, appearing in the opening first-class fixture at Southampton in 1905; his elder brother, Mark junior, turned out three times in 1932. Arthur was a regular from 1926 to 1936, scoring some handy runs and tasting success occasionally with his leg-spin, and then returned for a one-off season in 1947. The captain in that year, Arthur Childs-Clarke, summed Cox up as well as anyone: 'A great little trier.'

Although usually to be found in the supporting cast, he enjoyed some centre-stage moments in 1930. He scored his one and only first-class century, 104 against Nottinghamshire at Trent Bridge (completed with the last man, his great friend Reg Partridge, for company), and when Lancashire visited the County Ground he snatched four wickets in five balls, including a distinguished hat-trick of Ernest Tyldesley, Jack Iddon and Eddie Paynter. In the

same season he accounted for the young Don Bradman, having him caught at square leg for 35 when the Australians followed on in the tourist match at Northampton. Not a bad year for a 'bits and pieces' man.

He contributed 995 runs and 55 wickets in 1932, but 'lost' his bowling the following summer and struggled to find it again. With money even tighter than usual the club's committee decided they could do without Cox, who nevertheless rallied to Northamptonshire's colours in wartime games. In the first Robert Nelson Memorial Match at Spinney Hill in July 1941, he took 5-40 against the British Empire XI, his victims including journalist Reg Hayter and the team's founder, future MP Desmond Donnelly. The County won a narrow and emotional victory, of which Nelson would have been proud, by two runs on the day Japanese troops entered Saigon.

Called back for his 'bonus' year in 1947 he did not disgrace himself – 735 runs and 28 wickets – but that was the end of his first-class career. He stayed in the game, working as groundsman and coach at Northampton Grammar School, now Northampton School for Boys, and playing for the Vallence club in the early years of the Northamptonshire County League.

Brian Crump

RHB and RM, 1960-72

Born: Chell, Stoke-on-Trent, 25 April 1938				
Batting Career:				
M	**I**	**NO**	**Runs**	**HS**
317	473	108	8,652	133*
72	*55*	*8*	*691*	*74*
Ave	**100**	**50**	**ct/st**	
23.70	5	39	142	
14.70	*-*	*2*	*11*	
Bowling Career:				
Runs	**Wkts**	**Ave**		
19,938	807	24.70		
1,740	*87*	*20.00*		
BB	**5wi**	**10wm**		
7-29	30	5		
5-16	*1*	*-*		

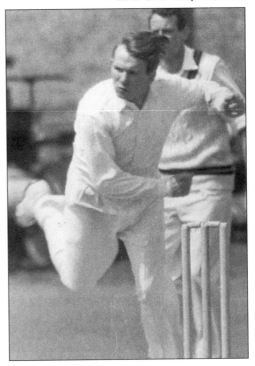

Dubbed 'The Atomic Pill' by the Essex players, Brian Crump was a pillar – albeit not a very tall one – of the Northamptonshire side in the 1960s. The son of Stan Crump, an outstanding Minor Counties cricketer with Staffordshire who was selected in his county's 'Team of the Century' in 2000, and cousin of the Steele brothers, Northamptonshire's David and Leicestershire's John, he produced some heroic performances with bat and ball.

Perhaps his finest cricketing moment came at Cardiff in August 1965. Northamptonshire and Glamorgan were both strongly in contention for County Championship honours, and Keith Andrew's men secured a tense 18-run victory which, at the time, looked to have given them a decisive advantage in the title race. Crump took 8-142 from 76.3 overs in the game, conceding less than two runs an over, and was carried into the pavilion when the final Glamorgan wicket went down, having bowled unchanged in the second innings. There was to be no happy ending to the story, of course, but Crump unquestionably earned his corn that summer, logging nearly 800 runs and 112 wickets at 19 apiece.

He topped the 100-wicket mark for the first time in 1963, as did the towering David Larter who stood some fifteen inches taller; shades of Hylda Baker and Cynthia. Crump had been steadily building his reputation as an all-rounder since his debut in 1960, but became that much more effective after Andrew experimented with the little man as a new-ball bowler. He may not have looked much like a quickie, but the figures told their own tale. At The Oval in 1963, Crump bowled Peter May for a single in what turned out to be the former England captain's final first-class appearance.

As a batsman, he managed five centuries – with a ten-year gap between the second and third – and made his best score of 133 not out against Warwickshire at Edgbaston in 1971. He was released at the end of his benefit year, 1972, but was still trundling away in club and over-50s cricket the best part of three decades later. Through his encouragement from an early age of Northamptonshire's current off-spinner Jason Brown, another Staffordshire boy and an England tour choice early in 2001, Brian Crump's influence has continued to be felt at Wantage Road.

Kevin Curran
RHB and RFM, 1991-99

Born: Rusape, Rhodesia (now Zimbabwe), 7 September 1959

Batting Career:

M	I	NO	Runs	HS
139	218	35	6,990	159
187	*173*	*36*	*4,144*	*119**
Ave	100	50	ct/st	
38.19	6	48	101	
30.25	*1*	*22*	*52*	

Bowling Career:

Runs	Wkts	Ave
8,180	271	30.18
5,371	*159*	*33.78*
BB	5wi	10wm
7-47	5	-
4-21	*-*	*-*

When, in the autumn of 1990, Northamptonshire beat a number of other counties in the race to sign Kevin Curran, club officials were confident they had a match-winner on their hands. The Zimbabwe-born all-rounder, who represented his native country in the World Cups of 1983 and 1987, had established his reputation as a hard-hitting batsman, hostile medium-fast bowler and fierce competitor during half a dozen summers with Gloucestershire. Expectations were accordingly high, and the Wantage Road faithful anticipated immediate results.

In fact, it took Curran a season or two to settle into his new surroundings. He found a kindred spirit in the captain, Allan Lamb, and excelled with the ball during the successful NatWest Trophy campaign of 1992. But it was to be nearly four years before he scored a Championship century for Northamptonshire, eventually getting to three figures in 1994 against Yorkshire at Luton.

'Be Positive' remained the Curran creed throughout his career, and he was always prepared to stand or fall by it. Sometimes, as at Canterbury in 1995 when he smashed a superb unbeaten 119 off 101 balls to secure a Sunday League victory, the buccaneer approach paid off; altogether less convincing was his much-discussed first-ball dismissal, stumped by a distance off Phil Tufnell, in a crucial Championship contest at Lord's in 1993.

Zimbabwe's elevation to Test status came too late for Curran, who became English-qualified in 1994 without attracting the selectors' attention. As his effectiveness as a bowler waned, so his batting became more disciplined, and he topped Northamptonshire's first-class averages with 1,242 runs at an average of nearly 60 in 1996, earning the club's Player of the Year award. Two years later he was handed the captaincy, in the hope that his outgoing personality and 'charge the guns' attitude would galvanise the team; the move was a failure, by any measure, and Curran lost the job within days of the season's end.

He did not figure in the plans of the new Director of Cricket, Bob Carter, and left the club at the end of 1999. It was a disappointingly low-key end to a Northamptonshire career which had begun, nearly a decade earlier, in an atmosphere of all-pervading optimism.

Percy Davis

RHB and occ. WK, 1935-52

Born: Brackley, Northants, 24 May 1915

Batting Career:

M	I	NO	Runs	HS
169	303	22	6,363	237
Ave	**100**	**50**	**ct/st**	
22.64	10	19	72/10	

Bowling Career:

Runs	Wkts	Ave
492	6	82.00
BB	**5wi**	**10wm**
2-13	-	-

Percy Davis was, quite simply, Northamptonshire through and through. A Brackley boy, he turned up for a trial at Wantage Road as an eighteen-year-old wearing breeches and leggings – his father was a stud groom – and was still on the scene more than thirty years later, captaining the County Colts and wondering why opposing captains objected when he used thirteen or fourteen players in a match. His devotion to his native county extended to donning the crimson Northamptonshire cap in the dressing room, before any other item of clothing.

Davis, whose younger brother Eddie played 104 times for Northamptonshire between 1947 and 1956, made his debut towards the end of his first season on the staff, 1935, against Essex at Northampton. A short man, looking like the jockey he nearly became, 'Sparrow' Davis hooked bravely, cut fiercely, and by 1939 his first team place was secure. He played a notable part in that summer's most memorable game, sharing a second-wicket stand of 176 with Dennis Brookes as Robert Nelson's team hammered Leicestershire inside two days – Northamptonshire's first Championship win for four years.

When cricket resumed after the war, Davis established himself as Brookes' regular opening partner. They posted 243 together against Worcestershire at Kidderminster in 1946, and the following year saw Davis plunder Somerset for a career-best 237 in six-and-a-half hours at Northampton. He passed 1,000 runs in each of the first three post-war summers, but then started to feel the draught of competition as the side was rebuilt. He dropped out of first-class cricket in 1952, and immediately embarked upon the next phase of his career, helping to bring through the new generation of Northamptonshire cricketers.

Davis remained on the club's coaching staff until 1967, when he accepted a job as coach at Harrow School. He continued to act as a scout for Northamptonshire, and also spent twenty-seven winters in South Africa, where his 'discoveries' at Dale College included Hylton Ackerman. A tremendously popular figure at the County Ground, he could still be seen following his old team's fortunes beyond his eightieth birthday – although, as John Watson pointed out in an appreciation of 'Sparrow' in the club's 1996 Yearbook, the seemingly immovable Northamptonshire cap had by then given way to a straw hat.

Winston Davis
RHB and RFM, 1987-90

Born: Sion Hill, St Vincent, 18 September 1958				
Batting Career:				
M	**I**	**NO**	**Runs**	**HS**
57	62	13	759	47
42	*25*	*7*	*244*	*34*
Ave	**100**	**50**	**ct/st**	
15.48	-	-	18	
13.56	*-*	*-*	*10*	
Bowling Career:				
Runs	**Wkts**	**Ave**		
5,776	208	27.76		
1,478	*40*	*36.95*		
BB	**5wi**	**10wm**		
7-52	13	4		
4-38	*-*	*-*		

Northamptonshire's search for an overseas fast bowler in the 1980s led them up more than one blind alley. The experiment with Kapil Dev was no long-term solution, while James Carse and Rupert 'Spook' Hanley had a season apiece without fitting the bill. Then, in 1987, the committee got what it wanted in the shape of Winston Davis from St Vincent. Tall and wiry, then out of favour with the West Indies selectors but with previous experience of the county circuit with Glamorgan, Davis had three productive summers with Northamptonshire.

Although usually competing with the likes of Michael Holding, Andy Roberts, Michael Marshall and Joel Garner for international recognition, Davis had stolen the limelight during the 1983 World Cup when he claimed 7-51 in a group match against Australia at Headingley. The following summer, taking leave of absence from Glamorgan to join the West Indian touring party as cover for the injured Marshall, he unexpectedly shone with the bat in the Old Trafford Test, hitting 77.

Davis was still only twenty-eight when he signed for Northamptonshire, and he captured 70 Championship wickets in his debut season – the best return for the County since Sarfraz Nawaz's 73 in 1977. He also appeared in the two Lord's finals of 1987, bowling the last over in the Benson & Hedges decider against Yorkshire; the opposition needed five runs from it to win, scored four, but took the silverware on fewer wickets lost in a tie. A couple of months later he removed Nottinghamshire openers Chris Broad and Tim Robinson to boost Northamptonshire's hopes of securing the NatWest Trophy, only for the game to slip away on the Monday courtesy of Richard Hadlee and a flurry of dropped catches.

Davis added 125 first-class wickets to his tally in the next two County Ground summers, but with Ambrose's star already in the ascendant he struggled for form in 1990 and was not re-engaged. All cricketing considerations then paled into insignificance in 1997 when an accident at home in St Vincent left Winston Davis a tetraplegic. His courage in adversity earned the admiration of the cricket world, and former colleagues, including many from Northamptonshire, were quick to support the fund-raising efforts on his behalf.

Jack Denton/Billy Denton
RHB and LB, 1909-19/ RHB,1909-24

Born: Rushden, 2 November 1890
Died: Rushden, 9 April 1971
Batting Career:

M	I	NO	Runs	HS
104	178	26	3,298	124
Ave	**100**	**50**	**ct/st**	
21.69	2	12	53	

Bowling Career:

Runs	Wkts	Ave
1,883	67	28.10
BB	**5wi**	**10wm**
5-39	2	-

Born: Rushden, 2 November 1890
Died: Bedford, 23 April 1979
Batting Career:

M	I	NO	Runs	HS
119	205	19	4,449	230*
Ave	**100**	**50**	**ct/st**	
23.91	4	16	54	

Bowling Career:

Runs	Wkts	Ave
42	0	-
BB	**5wi**	**10wm**
-	-	-

Born and bred in Rushden and educated at Wellingborough School, the identical Denton twins – William Herbert (Billy) and John Sidney (Jack) – made life well-nigh impossible for scorers and press men around the county circuit in the summers leading up to the First World War.

In 1910, against Nottinghamshire at Northampton, skipper 'Tim' Manning caused havoc, intentionally or otherwise, by swapping the pair over in the batting order. Legend has it that only the sharp eyes of Herbert Chapman, then manager of Northampton Town with his great years at Arsenal still ahead of him, spotted a slight difference in their footwork. The problem became even more acute in 1913 and 1914 when they regularly opened the innings together; indeed, in the latter year, two sets of twins, the Dentons and the Rippons, found themselves on opposing sides when Northamptonshire met Somerset.

Both men made their Northamptonshire debuts in 1909. Billy was thought the more solid batsman of the two, and secured a lasting place in the record books by carrying his bat for an unbeaten 230 against Essex at Leyton at 1913. It remained the County's highest Championship innings until Fred Bakewell surpassed it twenty years later. Jack's best knock was 124 off the Sussex bowlers at Hove in 1911; and on that same ground in 1914, the three Denton brothers – the twins plus Donald, six years their junior – all made half-centuries in Northamptonshire's then record total of 557-6 declared.

Jack and Billy were both taken prisoner in the war, while Donald, badly wounded, was left with an artificial leg. They all re-appeared for the County in 1919, Donald having been granted permission to bat with a runner, and Billy – who was proposed for the captaincy in 1922 but felt unable to accept – played on until 1924. Latterly, the County was prepared to pay the wages (£4 a week) of a man to take Billy's place in the shoe factory during his cricketing absences.

Mike Dilley

RHB and RFM, 1957-63

Born: Rushden, 28 March 1939
Batting Career:

M	I	NO	Runs	HS
33	38	16	232*	31*
1	*1*	*-*	*0*	*0*
Ave	100	50	ct/st	
10.54	-	-	13	
0.00	*-*	*-*	*-*	

Bowling Career:

Runs	Wkts	Ave
2,471	80	30.88
24	*2*	*12.00*
BB	5wi	10wm
6-74	2	-
2-24	*-*	*-*

Although his first-class career with Northamptonshire was relatively brief, 'Tex' Dilley created a record which remains unique in the club's annals; he performed the hat-trick twice in the space of six weeks during the summer of 1961. He then proceeded to dominate the local league scene to an unparalleled degree, and remains an interested follower of the game with an anecdote and an opinion for every occasion.

Another cricketer to emerge from the town of Rushden, Dilley joined the staff at Wantage Road in 1956 and made his Championship debut against Lancashire at Blackpool the following season. He shared the new ball with Frank Tyson but failed to take a wicket in his eleven overs. First team opportunities were few and far between until, in July 1961, with Tyson retired, Dilley received the call to play Nottinghamshire at Trent Bridge. In the first innings he removed Hugh Winfield, Cyril Poole and 'Bomber' Wells with successive balls, although the feat was spread over two overs and the bowler claimed he only knew what he had done when scorer Roy Smith congratulated him on board the team coach returning to the hotel!

Then at Hove, on 10 August, Dilley repeated the dose with the wickets of Les Lenham and Ted Dexter, both caught behind by Keith Andrew, either side of Ken Suttle, clean bowled. Dilley ended the summer with 43 wickets from 15 matches, but injury restricted his cricket to only four appearances in 1962 and eight in 1963. At the end of the latter season he failed to agree terms for a new contract and left the club. Much to his chagrin, Northamptonshire then refused to allow him to turn out in one-day games for Leicestershire.

Instead, he stacked up runs and wickets galore in the Northants County League, first for Rushden and then Irthlingborough, and captained both clubs to the league title. One of his new-ball partners at Irthlingborough was the up-and-coming Jim Griffiths. Dilley subsequently found a new lease of cricketing life in the 1990s with the County's Over-50s team, The Bullseyes.

John Dye

RHB and LFM, 1972-77

Born: Gillingham, Kent, 24 July 1942				
Batting Career:				
M	**I**	**NO**	**Runs**	**HS**
112	112	53	416	29*
117	*53*	*37*	*179*	*23*
Ave	**100**	**50**	**ct/st**	
7.05	-	-	18	
11.19	*-*	*-*	*15*	
Bowling Career:				
Runs	**Wkts**	**Ave**		
7,615	341	22.33		
3,392	*173*	*19.61*		
BB	**5wi**	**10wm**		
7-45	10	1		
5-30	*1*	*-*		

If John Dye had achieved nothing else in his six summers with Northamptonshire, he would still be remembered fondly by the club's supporters for his exploits on 4 September 1976. In the Gillette Cup final against Lancashire, the left-arm paceman produced a superb inswinging yorker to bowl Farokh Engineer before many of the spectators, including the author, had settled in their seats. Soon afterwards he got one to spit viciously and break Barry Wood's finger so badly that the key all-rounder not only retired hurt but was unable to bowl. Thus, with two crucial deliveries, 'Doc' Dye laid the foundations for a famous victory.

In seventeen seasons of first-class cricket – he played for Kent from 1962 to 1971 before heading north – Dye took 725 wickets costing under 24 runs apiece, frequently making early inroads with the new ball, just as on that September morning at Lord's. His amazing impact on the Northamptonshire attack was substantial and immediate; top of the County's averages in 1972 with 79 wickets at 18.06, forming a destructive partnership with Bob Cottam when the latter became available. Dye also proved highly effective in the limited-overs competitions, although he was spared the modern curse of the one-day

wide. As he later admitted: 'With my temperament, if I'd missed the leg stump by three inches and been called for a wide, I'd have gone loopy!'

Dye remained an integral member of the side to the end of 1976. Then, after losing his first team place in July 1977, he left Wantage Road in the midst of the so-called 'Great Schism'. Choosing to stay in his adopted county, he harvested many wickets in league cricket for Overstone Park and Isham, and became the much-respected coach at Wellingborough School, where his distinctive rolling run-up and comfortable bowling action could still be seen in the nets two decades after his county career ended.

The statistics would suggest that his prowess with the bat left a great deal to be desired. However, he surprised most observers, and possibly himself, by sharing in a last-wicket stand with Bishan Bedi worth 66 in 46 minutes against Worcestershire at Northampton in 1972. *Wisden* called it 'exciting.' 'Incredible' was the more common verdict.

William East

RHB and RM, 1895-1914

Born: Northampton, 29 August 1872
Died: Northampton, 19 December 1926

Batting Career:

M	I	NO	Runs	HS
157	261	34	3,913	86*
(113	151	20	2,757	117*)
Ave	**100**	**50**	**ct/st**	
17.23	-	12	75	
(21.05	2	9	62)	

Bowling Career:

Runs	Wkts	Ave	
10,233	493	20.75	
(6,643	423	15.70)	
BB	**5wi**	**10wm**	
7-11	28	4	
(9-80	29	5)	

For nearly twenty years, Billy East was Sancho Panza to George Thompson's Don Quixote. An accurate and, until health problems began to take their toll, tireless medium-pace bowler, and a reliable batsman at his best when runs were needed most, he shared countless battles with his fellow Northamptonian from 1895, when they both made their County debuts, until the First World War.

East hailed from the area of Northampton known as 'The Boroughs', now largely demolished, and learned his cricket in the street. 'There always seems to have been a bat and ball mixed up in my life,' he told a newspaper reporter after his retirement from the game. 'We played on the open road first, and I owe now for some of the windows I broke!' Not, perhaps, the most ambitious of men, East had to persuaded by Charlie Smith, the County's wicketkeeper, to forsake the lower levels of club cricket in the town and test his skills against better players.

He quickly proved himself in the Second-Class Counties competition, and it was entirely appropriate that in the final outing before elevation to first-class status, against Wiltshire at Trowbridge in August 1904, Thompson and East should bowl unchanged. On that occasion at least, East outdid his partner with 12-43 in the match against Thompson's 8-80.

East remained a force in Championship cricket and returned stunning figures of 7-11 as Lancashire collapsed from 69-2 to 114 all out at Northampton in 1911. But illness and injury began to sap his strength and resolve, and there was no possibility of him resuming his career after the war. Instead, he organised games for Lord Lilford and did odd jobs around the County Ground – coaching, collecting subscriptions and operating the scoreboard. East's benefit match, against Gloucestershire in 1907, had been badly affected by rain, and he was not a wealthy man. When he died, on the Sunday before Christmas in 1926, aged only fifty-four, he left his widow with a £36 mortgage on their home and no means of paying it off.

Happily, his friends rallied round and raised £500 to help the family. George Thompson was a pall-bearer at his funeral, and Lilford's wreath bore an inscription that summed up this much-loved Northampton character: 'He played the game.'

Alan Fordham
RHB, 1986-97

Born: Bedford, 9 November 1964				
Batting Career:				
M	**I**	**NO**	**Runs**	**HS**
167	297	24	10,939	206*
160	*153*	*3*	*4,588*	*132**
Ave	**100**	**50**	**ct/st**	
40.06	25	54	117	
30.59	*6*	*27*	*40*	
Bowling Career:				
Runs	**Wkts**	**Ave**		
297	4	74.25		
16	*1*	*16.00*		
BB	**5wi**	**10wm**		
1-0	-	-		
1-3	*-*	*-*		

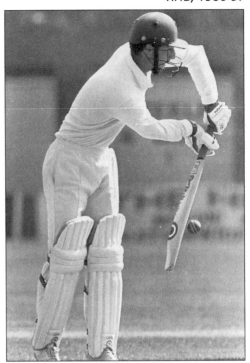

Alan Fordham spent much of his first season with Northamptonshire, as a nineteen-year-old just out of Bedford Modern School, skippering the County's Second XI. The perception of Fordham as the 'crown prince' persisted through much of his career, which saw him notch up nearly 11,000 first-class runs and 25 centuries for the club. But the first team captaincy proved elusive – he was passed over in favour of Rob Bailey in 1996 – and when he retired at the end of 1997, to take up an administrative role with the ECB, many supporters were left feeling that his talents had not been fully utilised at Northampton.

Fordham's initiation into County Championship cricket in 1986 was a painful affair, courtesy of a Clive Rice bouncer which struck him in the face. After finishing his studies at Durham University he became a 'full-timer' in 1988, and crossed a significant threshold the following season with 199 against Yorkshire at Sheffield. Northamptonshire named him their player of the year in 1990, when he amassed 1,767 runs and forged the 'F-Plan' opening partnership with his great friend, the former Somerset left-hander Nigel Felton. They became the 'New Firm' at the top of the order, replacing the 'Old Firm' of Geoff Cook and Wayne Larkins.

His enterprising approach brought him success in limited-overs cricket too. One of the few Northamptonshire batsmen to make a century in each of the three competitions, he carried off the Man of the Match award in the NatWest Trophy final of 1992 (after holding a breathtaking catch on the boundary to dismiss Neil Smith in the semi-final at Edgbaston), and took 101 off Australia's attack in a one-day contest at Northampton in 1993.

He reached 1,000 first-class runs for the fifth and final time in 1995, Northamptonshire's 'Tales of the Unexpected' season, only to lose form completely in 1996 after being appointed Bailey's deputy. His decision to exchange the Wantage Road dressing room for an office at Lord's was announced before the end of the 1997 campaign, and he signed off with an unbeaten 85 against Warwickshire at Edgbaston to ensure, much to his understandable satisfaction, a career average of 40.

Jim Griffiths

RHB and RFM, 1974-86

Born: Wellingborough, 13 June 1949				
Batting Career:				
M	**I**	**NO**	**Runs**	**HS**
177	138	51	290	16
164	*40*	*19*	*31*	*11**
Ave	**100**	**50**	**ct/st**	
3.33	-	-	36	
1.48	*-*	*-*	*15*	
Bowling Career:				
Runs	**Wkts**	**Ave**		
12,899	444	29.05		
4,937	*171*	*28.87*		
BB	**5wi**	**10wm**		
8-50	13	-		
5-43	*2*	*-*		

Anyone seeking an explanation for cricket's enduring appeal might usefully examine the career of Jim Griffiths. A talented seam bowler and a mainstay of Northamptonshire's attack for nearly a decade, with over 400 wickets to his credit, 'Big Jim' from Irthlingborough was also one of the game's least effective batsmen. In 138 first-class innings he failed to get off the mark no fewer than 51 times, including ten scoreless knocks in a row. Even his own testimonial brochure described him as 'The Wally of the Willow.'

Odd, therefore, that his finest hour should be a performance with the bat. In a never-to-be-forgotten NatWest Trophy semi-final in August 1981, Griffiths managed to withstand the pace of Michael Holding in the gathering gloom as Northamptonshire edged home against Lancashire by one wicket. He and Tim Lamb shared an unbroken stand of 13, and Griffiths was chaired off the field; a triumph for, arguably, the world's worst batsman against, unarguably, the world's best bowler. Richie Benaud interviewed him for BBC television immediately afterwards, and

Griffiths admits to answering each and every question with the single word 'Fantastic!' But no-one argued.

He made his debut in 1974 and was, until Duncan Wild and David Capel arrived on the scene a few years later, the only Northamptonshire-born player in the team. Leaving aside his batting heroics, he enjoyed his best season with the ball in 1981, taking 70 wickets including a career-best 8-50 against Glamorgan at Northampton. He led the County's averages the following summer, with 46 wickets at 26.09, and continued to pound in optimistically until 1986 when the club released him. He had already been granted a benefit – which, accordingly, became a testimonial – in 1987, and dispensing with his services at that moment was not one of Northamptonshire's most accomplished public relations exercises.

Understandably hurt at his treatment, Griffiths played a couple of seasons with Lincolnshire and then went back to his cricketing roots in the Northants County League. In 2000 he was still turning out for Irthlingborough at the age of fifty-one, remaining a sufficiently fierce competitor to mind very much indeed when slip chances went begging.

Roger Harper
RHB and OB, 1985-87

Born: Georgetown, British Guiana (now Guyana) 17 March 1963

Batting Career:

M	I	NO	Runs	HS
54	63	14	1,834	234
51	*41*	*10*	*791*	*65**
Ave	**100**	**50**	**ct/st**	
37.42	3	5	58	
25.52	*-*	*4*	*30*	

Bowling Career:

Runs	Wkts	Ave
4,188	137	30.56
1,512	*51*	*29.65*
BB	**5wi**	**10wm**
5-28	4	-
4-17	*-*	*-*

Stung by a couple of less than inspired overseas fast bowling signings, the Northamptonshire committee followed a different line of thought in 1985 and went for the tall Guyanese off-spinning all-rounder, Roger Harper. He had just made his way into the West Indies team and would, it was hoped, add a new dimension to a County side whose biggest problem at the time was dismissing the opposition twice.

In the usual way of things, Harper's immediate impact was with the bat and in the field rather than as a prolific wicket-taker. That first season saw him blaze a superb maiden century against Kent at Maidstone, smash a dominant Middlesex attack for 97 not out off 85 balls, including 8 sixes, in the next game at Uxbridge, and then hoist Rajesh Maru for six off the final ball of the match to beat Hampshire by one wicket at Southampton. His electric fielding was a revelation too. No wonder the 1985 Annual Report described him as 'a real crowd-pleaser.'

The acquisition of Nick Cook gave Harper a regular spin partner in 1986, and so impressed was the club by his maturity and cricket nous that he was appointed Geoff Cook's vice-captain. He topped Northamptonshire's first-class bowling averages with 62 wickets at 27.41, but once again his most notable contribution was as a batsman. Against Gloucestershire at the County Ground in May he made 234 in as many minutes with 12 sixes, one of which, in the general direction of Dennis Brookes' house in Wantage Road, must rank as one of the biggest hits ever seen at County headquarters.

Harper found himself in the cold for much of 1987 following the signing of Winston Davis. He became, in effect, the most brilliant and most expensive 'twelfthers' in the country, although his pick up and throw to end Graham Gooch's innings in the MCC Bicentenary match in August will live long in the memory. After visiting again with the West Indies in 1988, Harper opted to spend his English summers in the Lancashire League. He returned to the headlines early in 2000 by becoming coach of an ailing West Indian side – not, at that moment, the most enviable assignment in world cricket.

Rawlins Hawtin

RHB, 1902-30

Born: Bugbrooke, Northants,
1 February 1883
Died: Northampton, 15 January 1975
Batting Career:

M	I	NO	Runs	HS
85	150	5	3,558	135

(1 - did not bat)

Ave	100	50	ct/st
24.53	3	19	31

Bowling Career:

Runs	Wkts	Ave
-	-	-
-	-	-

BB	5wi	10wm
-	-	-
-	-	-

Like his near-contemporary, 'Tubby' Vials, Rawlins Hawtin could boast an involvement with Northamptonshire County Cricket Club spanning eight decades. He was chosen, as a nineteen-year-old, for the side to play Bedfordshire at Bedford in June 1902. At the club's AGM in 1971 he stood down after forty-four years on the committee, and retained an interest in the goings-on at Wantage Road until his death a few days short of his ninety-second birthday.

The younger brother of Roger Hawtin, an occasional for Northamptonshire before the First World War, Rawlins was born in Bugbrooke, a village near Northampton whose more recent inhabitants have included Alan Fordham and David Capel. Business commitments meant that his first-class career was a disjointed affair. Six years after his visit to Bedford, the County drafted him in to face Yorkshire in a lopsided contest which saw Northamptonshire swept away for 27 and 15 by George Hirst and Schofield Haigh. Much of Hawtin's life thereafter was devoted to the noble cause of making his

county a match for the Championship's traditional powers.

He played until 1911 and scored runs in his elegant style, then dropped out until 1919, was offered and declined the captaincy when Maurice Fitzroy stood down in 1927, and eventually signed off with a knock of 79 at Lord's in 1930, aged 47 years and 199 days. The record books show Jack Mercer and Lord Lilford as Northamptonshire's only older first-class cricketers, both in one-off matches.

As Jim Coldham noted of Hawtin: 'With him it was always business first, pleasure afterwards.' He could not afford to play more regularly, and caused a minor stir in 1921 when he intimated that he would require £10 in 'expenses' to turn out. But he gave far, far more to the game than he ever took from it. Hawtin was instrumental in founding the Northants Amateurs (still flourishing today) in 1925, and kept the county club ticking over during the Second World War. He served as club chairman from 1945 to 1953, chaired the old selection committee for thirteen years in two spells, and throughout, in the words of his obituary in the Northamptonshire yearbook, 'he neither sought praise nor publicity.'

Matthew Hayden
LHB, 1999-2000

Born: Kingaroy, Australia, 29 October 1971

Batting Career:

M	I	NO	Runs	HS
24	37	2	2,015	170
30	*30*	*3*	*1,071*	*107*
Ave	**100**	**50**	**ct/st**	
57.57	8	7	27	
39.67	*1*	*6*	*14*	

Bowling Career:

Runs	Wkts	Ave
148	5	29.60
73	*1*	*73.00*
BB	**5wi**	**10wm**
3-10	-	-
1-16	*-*	*-*

On the afternoon of 9 September 2000, Matthew Hayden received the County Championship's brand new Division Two trophy. He had become the first Northamptonshire First XI captain to lead his side to a league title since Tom Horton's men secured the Second-Class Counties Championship in 1904. It was a fitting reward for the tall left-hander from Queensland, who played a conspicuous role in a triumph which delighted the County's success-starved supporters.

Northamptonshire went into their penultimate match, against Essex at Wantage Road, needing just two bonus points to make certain of First Division cricket in 2001, and duly gained them on the opening day. But the ECB pitch liaison officer, Phil Sharpe, voiced concerns about the state of the strip and summoned a colleague, Alan Smith, to offer a second opinion. Hayden took his cue and scored a magnificent 164 in five and three quarter hours, pointedly raising his bat to the two-man panel at 50 and 100. The surface was exonerated, and the celebrations could begin.

Hayden joined Northamptonshire in 1999 to form a new leadership team with Director of Cricket Bob Carter. He possessed valuable knowledge of English conditions as a result of two tours, with the full Australian side in 1993 and Young Australia two years later, and then a summer with Hampshire in 1997, when he scored 2,426 runs in all competitions. His debut season with Northamptonshire, truncated by injury and an early return home to join his national squad, saw him head the County's first-class averages and, although not an experienced captain, he quickly gained the respect of his players by dint of his own performance.

He was even more impressive, as a batsman and a leader, in his second year, finishing with 1,270 Championship runs – nearly 500 more than anyone else in the side – and displaying greater imagination and flexibility in marshalling his resources on the field. Hayden also resurrected his Test career, which had begun with two cheap dismissals against South Africa at Johannesburg in March 1994. Overall, he had every reason to feel well-contented with his year's work in 2000; and if there was a spot of fishing and something cold to drink at the end of it all, so much the better.

Bob Haywood

RHB and RM, 1908-24

Born: Eltham, Kent, 16 September 1887				
Died: Edinburgh, 1 June 1942				
Batting Career:				
M	**I**	**NO**	**Runs**	**HS**
172	306	15	8,373	198
Ave	**100**	**50**	**ct/st**	
28.77	20	34	85	
Bowling Career:				
Runs	**Wkts**	**Ave**		
1,466	34	43.11		
BB	**5wi**	**10wm**		
3-73	-	-		

Some names – Brookes and Bakewell, Livingston and Lamb – crop up frequently in Northamptonshire's batting records; Robert Allnutt Haywood rather less so. But the tall, hard-hitting product of Captain McCanlis's famous Kent nursery at Tonbridge has figured for the last eighty years thanks to a golden summer in 1921 which saw him hit 8 centuries for the County. To date, no-one has matched, let alone improved upon, that tally.

Bob Haywood, both the son and father of first-class cricketers, came to the club in 1908 and turned out for Peterborough Town while qualifying by residence. Stepping up into the Northamptonshire side he attracted favourable notices in 1911, particularly after taking 121 off Yorkshire's attack at Dewsbury, and reached his 1,000 runs in both 1913 and 1914. He was already thirty-two when cricket resumed after the First World War in 1919, but the best was yet to come.

Emerging from a bus crash near Derby in the early part of the 1921 season with nothing worse than the odd bruise, Haywood proceeded to enjoy one of the great purple patches in Northamptonshire history. His 8 hundreds included a career-best 198 against Glamorgan at the County Ground, while Sussex were on the receiving end twice – 131 not out, carrying his bat, at Hove, and 164 at Northampton before Vallance Jupp knocked back his leg stump. Some people, however, are not easily satisfied: 'Haywood would easily be one of the finest batsmen in England, if only he would use his head better' wrote a national newspaper correspondent.

He finished off with 128 in the last game at Edgbaston, but his future with the club was by then in grave doubt. Haywood had been offered a lucrative coaching job at Fettes College; penurious Northamptonshire were unable to match the deal, and after that his appearances for the County were confined to a handful of fixtures during the school holidays. His departure, at the height of his powers, left a sizeable hole at the top of the order, not least because he was one of the few players in the team capable of wresting the initiative from opposing bowlers. Also a gifted rugby union forward, he remained in Scotland until his death at the early age of fifty-four.

Alan Hodgson

LHB and RFM, 1970-79

Born: Moorside, Consett, Co Durham, 27 October 1951				
Batting Career:				
M	**I**	**NO**	**Runs**	**HS**
99	118	24	909	41*
127	*76*	*19*	*414*	*26*
Ave	**100**	**50**	**ct/st**	
9.67	-	-	31	
7.26	*-*	*-*	*20*	
Bowling Career:				
Runs	**Wkts**	**Ave**		
5,964	206	28.95		
4,153	*169*	*24.57*		
BB	**5wi**	**10wm**		
5-30	2	-		
7-39	*2*	*-*		

One of so many Geordies to find a cricketing home in Northampton during the 1960s and 1970s, Alan Hodgson had his promising career as a seam bowler interrupted, and eventually truncated, by a serious back injury. Signed on by secretary Ken Turner as a sixteen-year-old straight from school in 1968, he made his first-class debut against Cambridge University two seasons later.

Hodgson initially faced fierce competition for a regular first-team berth from the likes of Bob Cottam, John Dye, Sarfraz Nawaz and, later, Jim Griffiths. But he played nearly a full summer in 1976, and enjoyed some particularly memorable moments that year in limited-overs cricket. He gained a Gillette Cup winners medal, and in the John Player League claimed 7-39 against Somerset – still Northamptonshire's best figures in the competition – including a hat-trick to finish off the match, much to the disgust of non-striker Brian Close. He again starred on a Sunday the following season with 6-22 against Derbyshire, and in the Championship helped Sarfraz dismiss Lancashire for 33 at the County Ground.

As a batsman he could hit freely, and enlivened an otherwise poor County showing against the 1973 New Zealanders with a robust 41 against Richard Hadlee, Dick Collinge and Bruce Taylor. His cheery knock was, admittedly, somewhat overshadowed by Glenn Turner completing his 1,000 runs before the end of May in the same match, the feat attracting much national publicity.

Hodgson remains Northamptonshire's leading wicket-taker in the Second XI Championship – 254 in 103 games, spread over twelve years – and after leaving the staff he became a major figure in the Northants County League, captaining the Old Northamptonians to the Premier title in 1983 and 1984. Eventually he returned to Wantage Road, where he ran the club shop and took charge of the County Colts side.

In 1998 he was appointed the first manager of the club's new £1.7 million indoor cricket centre, and found yet another important role as chairman of the Northamptonshire Cricket Board sub-committee charged with the task of overseeing league cricket in the county.

Tom Horton

RHB, 1895-1906

Born: Edgbaston, Birmingham, 16 May 1871				
Died: Bilton House, Rugby, 18 June 1932				
Batting Career:				
M	**I**	**NO**	**Runs**	**HS**
26	49	6	502	35
(115	*162*	*25*	*2,971*	*105)*
Ave	**100**	**50**	**ct/st**	
11.67	-	-	16	
21.69	*2*	*17*	*79*	
Bowling Career:				
Runs	**Wkts**	**Ave**		
4	0	-		
(751	*25*	*30.04)*		
BB	**5wi**	**10wm**		
-	-	-		
(3-32	*-*	*-)*		

Tom Horton was Northamptonshire's captain for eleven successive seasons, between 1896 and 1906. No one, before or since, has held the job for a longer period, and few of the County's other leaders down the years have been as greatly admired by team-mates, opponents and supporters alike as the Old Reptonian, whose school fellows included C.B. Fry and the elegant Palairet brothers, Lionel and Richard.

Although not quite in Fry's league as an all-round sportsman, Horton was multi-talented enough; a forceful batsman and sound fielder, an outstanding high-jumper and soccer player as a boy, and later a fearless rugby forward for Moseley and Midland Counties. As a leader on the cricket field, he relied on personality and persuasion rather than bull and bluster: 'Mr Horton is the least assertive of men, save perhaps when he gets a loose ball' noted a local reporter.

The ninth son of a Warwickshire landowner, he first appeared for the County in 1895 and took charge for the following season which saw Northamptonshire enter the Second-Class Counties – subsequently Minor Counties – competition, at that time unrecognised by the MCC. Horton's batting record was relatively modest but he had his moments, not least against the touring South Africans in 1901 when his unbeaten 102 in the second innings almost turned the match.

Horton was thirty-four when he led out Northamptonshire in the County's opening first-class game, at Southampton in May 1905. He described himself as 'a rather ponderous passenger' by that stage, but it would have been unthinkable for anyone else to have the asterisk next to his name on such a momentous day for the club. He retired at the end of 1906, and the professionals he had always looked after so well presented him with a smoking cabinet.

His business interests were varied – chairman of Atkinson's brewery, and a director of two large hotels in Birmingham – but he found time to take over the presidency of Northamptonshire from Lord Lilford after the ructions of 1921, and was one of the original four trustees of the Cockerill Trust, owners of the County Ground since 1923. His sense of duty had obliged him to volunteer as a tram driver in Birmingham during the First World War, and when he died in 1932 the club mourned the passing of a pivotal figure in its development.

Fred Jakeman

LHB, 1949-54

Born: Holmfirth, Yorks, 10 January 1920
Died: Huddersfield, 17 May 1986
Batting Career:

M	I	NO	Runs	HS
119	182	15	5,470	258*
Ave	**100**	**50**	**ct/st**	
32.75	10	27	36	

Bowling Career:

Runs	Wkts	Ave
162	5	32.40
BB	**5wi**	**10wm**
2-8	-	-

Another of Northamptonshire's post-war recruits from the north, Yorkshireman Fred Jakeman spent half a dozen seasons at Wantage Road, but in only one of them did he display with any consistency the full range of his considerable batting talents.

Jakeman had turned out a few times for his native county in 1946 and 1947, and then attracted the attention of Northamptonshire coach Jack Mercer, who hung around all evening outside a cinema in Nelson to catch a word with his target. The twenty-eight-year-old left-hander expressed 'fair shock' at the apparently less than generous terms initially offered by the club, but a deal was struck and he was eligible to play in 1949. He just missed out on 1,000 runs for Northamptonshire in his first two seasons, but put the record straight in 1951 by notching up 1,952 at 59.15. This left him fourth in the national batting averages, behind Peter May, Denis Compton and fellow left-hander, John Dewes.

His reputation for nervousness (one of the best-known Jakeman stories concerns him putting down his cigarette to go out and face Kent leg-spinner Doug Wright, and finding it still burning upon his return just a few moments later) was largely forgotten that year. He plundered six centuries, including 131 against the South Africans and an unbeaten 258, then a County record, in 320 minutes off the Essex attack, studded with 4 sixes and 35 fours. During July, he managed 558 runs without being dismissed: the scores were 80 not out, 258 not out, 176 not out and then, after missing two games, 44. His captain, Freddie Brown, described him in glowing terms as 'one of the hardest-hitting batsmen in the country.'

Disappointingly, he was never to rediscover that form. Troubled increasingly by fitness problems, Jakeman's average fell below 30 in 1952, and the following year he missed all but eight matches. His stock rose a little in 1954 with 135 in the opening Championship fixture against Sussex, but the improvement was not sustained, he lost his place in the side, and the club released him before the summer was out. His county career over, he returned to league cricket in Yorkshire before serving on the first-class umpires list from 1961 to 1972. Jakeman's son, Stuart, played three times for Northamptonshire in 1962 and 1963.

Ken James

RHB and WK, 1935-39

Born: Wellington, New Zealand, 12 March 1904
Died: Palmerston North, New Zealand, 21 August 1976

Batting Career:

M	I	NO	Runs	HS
101	178	17	3,428	105*
Ave	100	50	ct/st	
21.29	2	15	174/45	

Bowling Career:

Runs	Wkts	Ave
17	0	-
BB	5wi	10wm
-	-	-

One of the most gifted wicketkeepers New Zealand has ever produced, Ken James had two tours of both England and Australia and 11 Test appearances to his credit when he signed for Northamptonshire in 1935. His was to be a dual role, replacing the ageing Ben Bellamy behind the timbers and also acting as club coach. He stayed until the outbreak of war four years later.

James visited these shores on his country's behalf under Tom Lowry's captaincy in 1927 and 1931, and made such a favourable impression that several good judges were prepared to bracket him with Australia's Bert Oldfield and England's George Duckworth. *The Times* commented: 'He (James) is amazingly quick, very sure and at the same time keeps without semblance of fuss or of bother.' On these trips he executed many stumpings off the leg-spin of Bill Merritt; it was a partnership that would be renewed in due course at Wantage Road.

While qualifying for Championship cricket, James settled into his coaching duties. There was, inevitably, the odd failure; his attempts to alter left-arm spinner Cyril Perkins' line did the promising young bowler's confidence not a great deal of good. But James' own level of performance rarely dipped below excellent, and this was not only his wicketkeeping. He also scored valuable runs, including two centuries in 1938 against Derbyshire and Sussex, and occasionally opened the innings.

His stint with Northamptonshire coincided with some of the County's darkest days, and team-mates were glad of his cheerful and optimistic outlook. He had a hand – or two hands to be more precise – in one of the most celebrated dismissals of the period, holding the edge off Reg Partrdge which sent Don Bradman back to the pavilion for 2 when the 1938 Australians came to call. And, as the New Zealand cricket historian Dick Brittenden has pointed out, James' tally of catches and stumpings would have been considerably higher, had Northamptonshire managed to make their opponents bat twice more often!

After wartime service in the RAF – keeping wicket to Alec Bedser in a number of matches – Ken James returned to his native land, where he died in 1976.

Laurie Johnson
RHB and WK, 1958-72

Born: West Horsley, Surrey, 12 August 1936				
Batting Career:				
M	**I**	**NO**	**Runs**	**HS**
153	186	40	1,526	50
46	*30*	*9*	*177*	*31**
Ave	**100**	**50**	**ct/st**	
10.45	-	1	256/65	
8.43	*-*	*-*	*42/3*	
Bowling Career:				
Runs	**Wkts**	**Ave**		
61	1	61.00		
BB	**5wi**	**10wm**		
1-60	-	-		

Abundant patience is a prerequisite for reserve wicketkeepers, and few have endured a longer wait for their regular first-team opportunity than Laurie Johnson. At his native Surrey, the whimsical Johnson was third in line, behind Arthur McIntyre and Roy Swetman. So in 1958 he moved to Northamptonshire, where only Keith Andrew stood in his way. Andrew, however, missed precious few games until his retirement in 1966, leaving his understudy to set Second XI records (401 victims in 183 games) that will never be beaten and get just just an occasional chance to shine at the higher level.

But shine he did. Twice, against Sussex at Worthing in 1963 and against Warwickshire at Edgbaston two years later, he claimed ten dismissals in a match. When Andrew finally departed the scene, Johnson was the County's first choice for four summers until the arrival of George Sharp, who was fourteen years younger and a more accomplished batsman. Johnson's productive days with the bat were, frankly, few and far between. Famously, in 1959, he was run out first ball at The Oval after being sent in as nightwatchman to 'protect' Dennis Brookes. The incident reportedly prompted a rare expletive from the lips of the captain, Raman Subba Row, usually the most mild-mannered of men.

Johnson met and married a Northampton girl shortly after joining the County club, and his sense of loyalty belongs to a bygone, less avaricious age. Although Sharp was in possession by 1972, Johnson received the call to play against the Australian tourists in August, and contributed to Northamptonshire's historic seven-wicket victory with two catches and a stumping, all off Bishan Bedi in the second innings. It was his final first-class appearance, and a splendid way to bow out.

A fine golfer and an even better raconteur, Johnson has enlivened many a Former Players' Reunion with the story of his disaster as nightwatchman, not to mention Donald Carr ordering former Northampton groundsman Bert Brailsford to bring out a vacuum cleaner instead of a roller to deal with a particularly dusty strip, and the discovery that Freddie Brown's 'W-and-W' on the drinks list stood not for whisky and water, but for whisky and whisky.

Vallance Jupp
RHB and OB, 1923-38

Born:	Burgess Hill, Sussex, 27 March 1891				
Died:	Spratton, Northants, 9 July 1960				

Batting Career:

M	I	NO	Runs	HS
280	477	29	13,653	197
Ave	**100**	**50**	**ct/st**	
30.47	15	77	118	

Bowling Career:

Runs	Wkts	Ave
24,075	1,078	22.33
BB	**5wi**	**10wm**
10-127	79	15

Anyone doubting Vallance Jupp's status as one of the great all-rounders in cricket history should be referred to the pages of *Wisden*. He performed the 'double' on no fewer than ten occasions; only Wilfred Rhodes and George Hirst stand ahead of him. In six seasons, 1925 to 1928 inclusive plus 1931 and 1932, he achieved this feat in Northamptonshire matches only. A cricketer of the highest quality, he was, in common with the County's two other towering figures of the inter-war years, Fred Bakewell and 'Nobby' Clark, emphatically not the answer to a timid committee man's prayers.

Jupp began his career as a professional with his native Sussex before the First World War, turned amateur in 1919 and joined Northamptonshire as player-secretary following the 'coup' instigated by Stephen Schilizzi in the autumn of 1921 – a year which saw Jupp appear twice for England against Australia as one of the thirty men chosen during the summer by the increasingly bewildered selectors. The new appointee had plenty of time to concentrate

on fixture lists and minutes as he was not eligible for Championship cricket until 1924. But he soon made up for lost time, and at a stroke Northamptonshire became a stronger and more competitive side. Having converted from pace to off-spin during his Sussex days, he captured 110 wickets in 1925 including a match haul of 15-52, with a hat-trick in the first innings, against Glamorgan at Swansea. A year later he weighed in with a County-best 197 off Worcestershire's attack at New Road.

Such was the nature of his 'amateur' arrangement that the club reflected its delight with his performances on the field by increasing his salary as secretary to £500 a year in 1927. When Maurice Fitzroy stood down as captain midway through that season, and Rawlins Hawtin was unable to spare the time to succeed him, Jupp took charge. Subsequent events lead one to the unavoidable conclusion that this was not a happy decision.

Within a few months he and the committee were at loggerheads over Jupp's insistence that a masseur accompany the team on away trips. Too costly, the worthy gentlemen retorted. Shortly afterwards he was reprimanded for absenting himself from a match without permission, and the committee then wheeled him in a couple of times to express disquiet over some of his expenses claims. His disputes with 'Nobby' Clark were becoming both more frequent and more toxic. And while the difficulties mounted, Jupp just kept on scoring runs and taking wickets.

Matters came to a head in September 1931. A decade after the stormy meeting that had precipitated his employment, another led to his resignation as both captain and secretary. Past his fortieth birthday by now, he played on under 'Beau' Brown in 1932 and demonstrated that he had lost little if any of his skill by recording Northamptonshire's first, and so far only, 'all-ten' in first-class cricket – 10-127 in 39 overs against Kent at Tunbridge Wells. That winter, writing in the *Sunday Dispatch*, Jupp firmly backed Douglas Jardine's captaincy in Australia and attacked the 'pernicious press campaign' against him.

He could be a most convivial companion. Alex Snowden recalled an eventful journey to a game in the 1930s which saw Jupp entertain the locals at a pub in Guildford by sticking a pin through the hard skin on his spinning finger, come out with 'one comic tale after another', arrive an hour and a half late for the start of play and then curse Ben Bellamy, the senior pro, for losing the toss. But tragedy struck one January night in 1935 when Jupp was involved in a road accident which led to the death of a motorcyclist and his own imprisonment for manslaughter.

He returned to county cricket in 1936 and continued to turn out for Northamptonshire until 1938. 'He would spin his slow-medium off-breaks round the wicket tirelessly and with mature cunning,' wrote Dudley Carew, 'and his batting gave some sort of stability and backbone to an amorphous and uncertain whole.'

Proposed by 'Tubby' Vials, Jupp stood for election to the club's committee at the 1949 Annual Meeting. Perhaps the irony was not lost on those with memories of his regular run-ins with that august body; he lost the vote.

Vallance Jupp – a great all-rounder by any measure.

63

Jim Kingston

RHB and LB, 1878-92

Born: Northampton, 8 July 1857
Died: Naples, Italy, 14 March 1929
Batting Career:

M	I	NO	Runs	HS
-	-	-	-	-
Ave	100	50	ct/st	
-	-	-	-	

Bowling Career:

Runs	Wkts	Ave
-	-	-
BB	5wi	10wm
-	-	-

See statistical note on page 4.

Jim Kingston was truly a Northamptonshire cricketing pioneer: a key figure in the organisation of the County club in 1878, its first captain and, later, its first paid administrator. The second of schoolmaster William Kingston's nine sons, eight of whom played for Northamptonshire, Jim was also a poet, composing odes on great occasions ranging from the death of Disraeli to W.G. Grace's birthday, and a frequent writer of letters to the press on a variety of pet subjects including – somewhat radically – government financial backing for sport.

He followed his elder brother Fred (a member of the celebrated Cambridge University XI of 1878) into the pre-reformation County side in 1875, and three years later he hit 128 for the Gentlemen of South Northamptonshire against their northern counterparts on the Racecourse. That same evening, 31 July 1878, he joined other local luminaries at the momentous meeting in Northampton's George Hotel which led to the election of the 'new' club's first committee. This body was made up of sixteen members, including twenty-one-year-old Jim.

He remained captain for the next nine summers and, after a two year gap, took charge again in 1890 and 1891, managing to combine cricket with his professional life as a solicitor. He led Northamptonshire against Surrey Club and Ground in May 1886, the inaugural fixture at the County Ground. This was very much a family affair: brother Fred faced the first ball, two other Kingstons (Bert and Walter) were in the side, and their father William proposed a lunchtime toast.

Jim became the club's paid secretary in 1891, but the appointment was not a success. The finances were in a mess when he took up the post and, with the deficit deepening daily – not helped by the long-serving ground bowler, Joe Potter, threatening legal action to obtain settlement of his wages arrears – the secretary resigned. He played his final game for Northamptonshire at Stoke-on-Trent in 1892, then moved to Birmingham on business and, ironically, made his only appearance in first-class cricket for Warwickshire, against Leicestershire in 1894. After the early death of his wife, Jim emigrated to Italy to teach English and lived out his last quarter of a century there.

Billy Kingston

RHB, 1894-1909

Born: Northampton, 12 August 1874
Died: Northampton, 17 February 1956

Batting Career:

M	I	NO	Runs	HS
77	140	2	2,594	83
(101	*149*	*13*	*3,941*	*163)*
Ave	**100**	**50**	**ct/st**	
18.79	-	8	44	
(28.98	*6*	*18*	*81)*	

Bowling Career:

Runs	Wkts	Ave
25	2	12.50
BB	**5wi**	**10wm**
2-5	-	-

When George Thompson took guard to face Northamptonshire's opening delivery in first-class cricket, from Hampshire's Henry Persse in 1905, the man at the non-striker's end was W.H. 'Billy' Kingston, the eighth of the nine famous brothers and one of only two of them – along with the baby of the family, H.E., known as 'Tim' – to appear in the County Championship for Northamptonshire.

He made his County debut against Surrey Second XI at The Oval in 1894, batting at number six, but found himself promoted to open in the next match and remained at the top of the order for most of his career. An adaptable player who usually sold his wicket dearly, Billy hit his maiden century for Northamptonshire off Berkshire's bowlers in 1898, and in the course of his 149 was called upon to act as 'third umpire.' An appeal went up for a catch against his partner, Tom Brown; both officials claimed to be unsighted; Kingston was consulted, sided with the fielder, and Brown went on his way.

Billy scored runs consistently as Northamptonshire established their formidable reputation in the Second-Class Counties competition, and in 1904 he proved himself capable of succeeding against the very best. On a rain-damaged pitch at Stoke-on-Trent in July, he made 102 against a Staffordshire attack led by the great S.F. Barnes. Just two days later, Billy was heading for The Oval to open the innings for the Gentlemen, captained by 'Ranji', against the Players. Warwickshire's Sam Hargreave bowled him for 5, and he wasn't required to try again as the Gents – also including B.J.T. Bosanquet, fresh from his Australian triumphs, and Billy Murdoch – won by an innings.

Billy made the step up with his Northamptonshire colleagues the following season, but averaged below 19 in his 140 first-class knocks for the County. Only in 1908, with 989 runs, did he approach his best form.

It became more difficult for him to spare the time for cricket – he was, for many years, a sports outfitter in Northampton – and he played his last match in 1909. Interestingly, the family's connection with the club was perpetuated in 1999 when Billy's great-grandson, Will Kingston, worked in the catering department at Wantage Road.

Anil Kumble

RHB and LB, 1995

Born: Bangalore, India, 17 October 1970				
Batting Career:				
M	**I**	**NO**	**Runs**	**HS**
17	21	5	321	40*
19	*8*	*2*	*24*	*8*
Ave	**100**	**50**	**ct/st**	
20.06	-	-	11	
4.00	*-*	*-*	*5*	
Bowling Career:				
Runs	**Wkts**	**Ave**		
2,143	105	20.40		
685	*30*	*22.83*		
BB	**5wi**	**10wm**		
7-82	8	2		
4-50	*-*	*-*		

When Anil Kumble met the local press for the first time on a freezing cold Saturday morning at the County Ground in April 1995, he was clad in as many sweaters and tracksuits as he could lay his hands on, all fresh out of their wrappers. He could have been forgiven for wondering if this was really such a good idea. Five months later, the tall, polite bowler from Bangalore was on his way home after capturing 105 first-class wickets at 20.40 apiece and pushing Northamptonshire to within touching distance of that elusive first Championship title. As short-term signings go, he must rank as the County's best one ever.

Whipping through his top-spinners at approaching medium-pace, 'Apple Crumble' proved even more devastating in Championship cricket than captain Allan Lamb and coach Bob Carter had hoped. He was aided that summer by some excellent close catching, particularly in the crucial positions at short leg and silly point, and thanks to the efforts of Lamb and the other batsmen he generally had a decent total behind him. This was never more so than in one of the most bizarre games Wantage Road has ever seen: Nottinghamshire 527 and 157, Northamptonshire 781-7 declared to win by an innings and 97 runs, Kumble taking nine wickets for 161 from 89.1 overs in the match.

He became the first bowler to reach 100 wickets in an English season since Neil Foster and Waqar Younis in 1991, and the first to achieve the feat for Northamptonshire since his fellow Indian, Bishan Bedi, in 1973. It was entirely characteristic of Kumble that within half an hour of reaching the milestone he should be found chatting during the lunch interval with budding leg-spinners from the County's youth squads.

Kumble made his Test debut against England at Old Trafford in 1990, and his first victim was none other than Allan Lamb. He joined the cricketing immortals on 7 February 1999 by claiming 10-74 against Pakistan in Delhi – only the second 'all ten' in Test history, after Jim Laker's destruction of Australia in 1956. Kumble returned to the Championship scene with Leicestershire in 2000, but never threatened to repeat his triumphs of 1995.

M	I	NO	Runs	HS
284	452	74	20,128	235
314	*299*	*40*	*10,155*	*132**
Ave	**100**	**50**	**ct/st**	
53.24	56	100	218	
39.21	*14*	*60*	*92*	

Born: Langebaanweg, South Africa, 20 June 1954

Batting Career:

Bowling Career:

Runs	Wkts	Ave
165	7	23.57
23	*2*	*11.50*
BB	**5wi**	**10wm**
2-29	-	-
1-4	-	-

Allan Lamb became a master at transforming the improbable into cricketing reality. A lost cause, a game fizzling out, a target out of reach; all these scenarios would present Lamb with an irresistible challenge. And the longer he played, the more likely he was to meet that challenge successfully.

In 1995, the last of his eighteen seasons with Northamptonshire and his first and only one in sole charge of first-team affairs, he presided over a dozen Championship victories, some of which bore the unmistakable imprint of his own personality – enterprising, ebullient, almost hectoring the opposition into doing what he wanted them to do. He scored his own runs (1,237 at 56.22) quickly, leaving more time for Anil Kumble to wear down the other team's batsmen, and apart from third place in the Championship he also steered Northants into the final of the NatWest Trophy, a game which turned on a crucial umpiring decision in favour of his Warwickshire counterpart, Dermot Reeve. There was no cigar at the end of it all, but it was a summer no County supporter lucky enough to be around at the time will ever forget.

And then, suddenly, he was gone. Lamb had already decided to hand over the captaincy for 1996, and in March he announced his retirement as a player to ward off possible TCCB censorship of his forthcoming autobiography. The new skipper and chief coach, Rob Bailey and John Emburey, learned of this while in South Africa on the team's pre-season tour; this was a final surprising twist in a career laden with them.

Lamb was not Northamptonshire's first choice when they sought an overseas batsman for 1978. They tried for another South African, Peter Kirsten, and only when he dropped out of the reckoning did they agree terms, through their emissary Roy Barker, with the twenty-three-year-old from Western Province. Secretary Ken Turner later remarked of Lamb: 'Those who are born Cavaliers can never be turned into Roundheads.' It was soon apparent that the man from The Fairest Cape (albeit with English-born parents, which helped his cause when it came to Test qualification) had more in common with Prince Rupert than Henry Ireton. And yet there was something almost Cromwellian in his relentless efficiency at county level; Lamb's average of 53.24 for just over 20,000 runs puts him more than seven runs an innings ahead of the next 'regular' in the list, Jock Livingston. His tally of

Allan Lamb hits out in the 1980 Benson & Hedges Cup final, which ended in Northamptonshire's victory over Essex by 6 runs.

56 centuries for Northamptonshire is second only to Dennis Brookes' 67.

Lamb appeared in 79 Test matches for England between 1982 and 1992 and 122 limited-over internationals (which are both easily County records). Highlights included six centuries against the West Indies, three of them in the 1984 series, and hitting 18 off Bruce Reid's final over to beat Australia in a one-dayer at Sydney in 1986/87.

He averaged 36 in Tests, which left him outside the very top rank of England players down the years, and occasionally the selectors decided to look elsewhere. The next set of county bowlers to come up against him would invariably find themselves on the receiving end of his indignation, most spectacularly in 1986 when he took 157 off Imran Khan and company on a difficult pitch at Hastings to earn Northamptonshire an astonishing one-wicket win over Sussex.

The following year he clinched an equally unlikely victory in the Benson & Hedges Cup semi-final at Canterbury. Lamb's unbeaten 126 off 101 balls, described by match adjudicator Denis Compton as 'one of the best limited-over innings ever', made light of an asking rate which had risen to nearly ten runs an over. In 1992 he shrugged off the bitter controversy surrounding his newspaper revelations about alleged ball-tampering to lead the County to the NatWest Trophy, thrashing Leicestershire in the final.

Lamb took time to grow into the Northamptonshire captaincy, which he inherited from Geoff Cook in 1989. In truth, the previous year had marked the real start of 'The Lamb Era' as the County basked in the national spotlight after signing Dennis Lillee, and Lamb himself embarked on Northamptonshire's first 'showbiz' benefit, drawing on his many entertainment and sporting contacts from around the world. The days of darts matches in Duston and bat raffles in Braunston were well and truly over. In fund-raising, as on the cricket field, Allan Lamb was always thinking big and aiming high.

Wayne Larkins
RHB and RM, 1972-91

Born: Roxton, Beds, 22 November 1953

Batting Career:

M	I	NO	Runs	HS
363	628	43	20,317	252
352	*338*	*19*	*9,592*	*172**

Ave	100	50	ct/st	
34.72	44	85	213	
30.07	*16*	*50*	*103*	

Bowling Career:

Runs	Wkts	Ave
1,711	40	42.77
2,397	*77*	*31.12*

BB	5wi	10wm
5-59	1	-
5-32	*1*	-

Some say it was David Graveney who coined it, others say Jonathan Agnew. Either way, a new verb appeared in the cricketing lexicon during the 1980s: to ned, as in 'I don't want to bowl any more, captain, I have been well and truly nedded.' In time, it was adopted by most purveyors of the new ball obliged to confront Northamptonshire opener Wayne 'Ned' Larkins. Its use has been confined in recent years to the Minor Counties circuit, following Larkins' return to his native Bedfordshire.

Without question one of the most exciting English players of his generation, he was a guaranteed bar-emptier around the county circuit. If the first delivery of the match was pitched up and Larkins felt in fighting trim, it would rebound off the boundary boards a second or two later. It disappointed his many supporters that the international arena never saw the best of this richly gifted batsman; his 13 Tests spread over eleven years yielded only three half-centuries, although the selectors were never willing to give him the 'run' in the side that might have done wonders for his confidence.

Larkins' Northamptonshire career was almost stillborn. Signed on at £7 a week (plus accommodation) in 1969, he made his debut in 1972 and played a total of 25 first-class matches in three seasons – with an average of 9.75, including a hundred against Cambridge University! The County's current Chief Executive, Stephen Coverdale, remembers keeping wicket in a Second XI match around this time with Larkins batting: 'One could sense his insecurity. In his mannerisms – the tentative shuffling at the wicket – it was clear that things were not right.'

Salvation arrived at Chelmsford one day in August 1975. Batting at number five and coming to the crease at 21-3 in the County's second innings, Larkins hit 127 and shared in a fourth-wicket stand worth 273 with Mushtaq Mohammad. A year later he was enjoying the celebrations at Lord's after Northamptonshire's Gillette Cup triumph over Lancashire, and the retirement of Roy Virgin in 1977 allowed him to go in first on a regular basis, partnering Geoff Cook.

They enjoyed batting together, and managed to convey that enjoyment to spectators. Reflecting on his lengthy association with Larkins, Cook recalls their

Left: *Wayne Larkins warms up for another season at Wantage Road.* Right: *The Old Firm – Wayne Larkins (right) with Geoff Cook.*

joint approach: 'A nasty twenty minutes last thing at night? No worries, more a chance for a rapid 30 while the fielders are around the bat. How did we ever fail? It must have been the others' fault!' Against Lancashire at Wantage Road in 1986, Northamptonshire were closing in on an easy win – the victory target being only 33. But West Indian paceman Patrick Patterson was not about to concede without a fight, and bowled two of the quickest overs seen in Northampton for many a season. Larkins took him on in equally thrilling fashion, steering a six over third man. A wry smile never left the lips of Cook, watching from the non-striker's end. It was wonderful stuff.

Larkins passed 1,000 runs for the County in each of the eight summers between 1978 and 1985, blazing his way to two double-centuries – 236 at Derby and 252 at Swansea – in the space of seven weeks during 1983.

This might have earned him another England chance, but for the fact that he was then serving a three-year ban from Test cricket for joining the 1982 'rebel' tour to South Africa. The last of his 44 three-figure scores for Northamptonshire was also a 'double'; 207 against Essex in 1990.

At the end of the following season, seeking a new challenge, he threw in his lot with Durham. His stint in the north-east was to end amid unpleasantness in 1995, but he at least had the satisfaction of completing a 'set' of centuries against the pre-1992 first-class counties when he hit 112 against Northamptonshire on his old home patch. Since joining Bedfordshire in 1996 he has raised his tally of Lord's cup finals to ten; seven with Northamptonshire and two with the minor county, plus the World Cup decider against the West Indies in 1979.

Born: Inverness, 24 April 1940
Batting Career:

M	I	NO	Runs	HS
134	128	47	517	51*
26	*16*	*6*	*60*	*27*
Ave	**100**	**50**	**ct/st**	
6.38	-	1	43	
6.00	*-*	*-*	*3*	

Bowling Career:

Runs	Wkts	Ave
9,295	511	18.19
782	*48*	*16.29*
BB	**5wi**	**10wm**
8-28	24	5
5-24	*1*	*-*

When Northamptonshire near as dammit won the County Championship title in 1965, they owed much to their towering fast bowler, David Larter. Although called up for three of that summer's six Tests, the 6 ft 7 in paceman collected 74 County wickets at 13.59, including match hauls of 12-56 and 12-80 in successive games during June, against Somerset and Yorkshire respectively. Larter's immediate reward was a second tour to Australia in 1965/66; but, sadly, his Northamptonshire career was virtually over.

He broke down with an ankle injury early in 1966, suffered a relapse in April 1967 after a Gillette Cup match at Luton, and announced his retirement at the age of twenty-seven. His brief return in 1969, claiming 14 wickets in three Championship outings and bowling economically in the new Sunday League, served to underline what a major loss he was to Northamptonshire. The figures strongly support that view; in all first-class cricket he finished with 666 wickets in 182 matches, taking them at less than 20 runs apiece.

Larter joined the County from Framlingham College in 1959, and even during that first summer in the Second XI there were ominous murmurings in committee about the need to use him sparingly and not

place undue strain on his tall frame. He made his first team debut at Derby in June 1960, opening the attack with Frank Tyson – a fascinating juxtaposition of the old and the new. By 1962 he was attracting the attention of the England selectors, and made a spectacular start to his Test career with 5-57 and 4-88 in the final Test of the summer against Pakistan.

He went along on Ted Dexter's 1962/63 expedition Down Under more or less for the ride, not getting a Test until New Zealand, but he came home to enjoy his best season in 1963 – 112 wickets for Northamptonshire, plus a hat-trick in the Gillette Cup semi-final against Sussex. His productivity showed no signs of waning over the next couple of years, until the injury nightmare began.

Off the field, Larter was far from a snarling fire-breather. Team-mates remember his fondness for a nap in the dressing room. But with a cricket ball in his hand he set a stiff examination for county and international batsmen, albeit for a disappointingly brief period.

Albert Lightfoot

LHB and RM, 1953-70

Born: Woore, Shropshire, 8 January 1936				
Batting Career:				
M	**I**	**NO**	**Runs**	**HS**
290	489	59	11,837	174*
31	*29*	*4*	*474*	*84**
Ave	**100**	**50**	**ct/st**	
27.52	12	59	160	
18.96	*-*	*2*	*9*	
Bowling Career:				
Runs	**Wkts**	**Ave**		
5,980	167	35.80		
72	*1*	*72.00*		
BB	**5wi**	**10wm**		
7-25	4	-		
1-18	*-*	*-*		

Ask any Northamptonshire follower of a certain age about Albert Lightfoot and you are guaranteed to hear not about the 12,000-odd runs he did make for the County, but about the one run he didn't. Against Richie Benaud's 1961 Australians, Northamptonshire mounted a spirited challenge after being left to score 198 for victory in two and a half hours, and Lightfoot's gallant half-century helped reduce the target to four runs off the final over. With one ball to go, the scores were level. Alan Davidson bowled to Malcolm Scott who missed, but set off for a bye to acting-wicketkeeper Bobby Simpson; Lightfoot, inexplicably, stayed put at the non-striker's end, Scott was run out, and the Aussies escaped with a draw.

This brainstorm aside, Northamptonshire's own Shropshire Lad gave valuable service for nearly twenty years as a player, before extending his stay at Wantage Road as head groundsman between 1973 and 1978.

Signed in 1953 principally as a medium-fast bowler, Lightfoot soon emerged as a talented left-handed batsman who made his breakthrough in 1958 with a maiden century against Surrey at The Oval, helping Raman Subba Row add a record-breaking 376 for the sixth wicket. 'If he continues to improve, he may well reach the highest class' noted that season's Annual Report, but in the event he was never to progress beyond the county scene.

Lightfoot's most productive batting season was 1962, when he scored 1,795 runs for Northamptonshire including 5 hundreds, and he revived his career at the end of the decade by also reaching 1,000 runs in both 1968 and 1969. In between he contributed some useful performances, although colleagues felt a lack of 'drive' often held him back. He also took a physical knock or two, not least in the last Championship match staged at Rushden, against Lancashire in 1963, when a ball from Brian Statham reared up off the less than ideal pitch and struck Lightfoot on the nose.

He took a benefit in 1970, having already informed the club that he was not intending to see re-engagement at the end of the summer, only to exchange his bat for the heavy roller at the County Ground three years later.

Lord Lilford
RHB, 1911

Born: Lilford Hall, Northants, 12 January 1863
Died: Kettering, 17 December 1945
Batting Career:

M	I	NO	Runs	HS
1	1	-	4	4
Ave	**100**	**50**	**ct/st**	
4.00	-	-	-	

Bowling Career:

Runs	Wkts	Ave
-	-	-
BB	**5wi**	**10wm**
-	-	-

Make no mistake – John Powys, fifth Baron Lilford, does not earn his place in this volume as a result of scoring 4 in his only first-class match, at the age of forty-eight, against All India at Northampton in 1911. His inclusion is based on the not insignificant fact that, but for his energy and generosity in the early years of the last century, it is doubtful whether Northamptonshire would have been able to retain first-class status, and very possibly would not have achieved it in the first place.

When Lilford succeeded the 5th Earl Spencer (the 'Red Earl' of successive Gladstone governments) as the club's president in 1903, he immediately donated £100 from his own pocket, the first of so many contributions either in cash or kind. A year later he launched 'The Lord Lilford County Cricket Fund' to finance Northamptonshire's promotion to the County Championship, and was never afraid to use his considerable social clout – as an alderman, landowner and Freemason – to obtain support from other prominent individuals.

His passion for the game extended, reportedly, to carrying a ball about with him in case there was the opportunity of some fielding practice. He laid on splendid country house cricket at Lilford Hall, near Oundle, with lengthy intervals for luncheon (*not* lunch), plenty of home-brewed ginger beer served in champagne magnums, and shiny red apples from the estate for those who performed well. Alex Snowden, an 'occasional' for Lilford's XI, recalled: 'The wicket was first-class ... [and] to add to the colourful scene, there were always some of Lady Lilford's multi-hued macaws flying through the trees.' His solitary appearance for Northamptonshire's first team was a happy gesture on the club's part, although he was undoubtedly past his physical peak by that stage – 'as round as a pea' according to a rhyme popular among the boys at Wellingborough School.

Lilford remained as president until 1921, when he resigned ('no gentleman in the room could expect me to do otherwise') in the aftermath of a particularly stormy special General Meeting. But he did not walk away, staying on the committee for another fifteen years and still bolstering the coffers when the need arose. His obituary did not appear in *Wisden* until Matthew Engel rectified the oversight in 1994.

Leonard 'Jock' Livingston

LHB and occ. WK, 1950-57

Born: Sydney, Australia, 3 May 1920
Died: Sydney, Australia, 16 January 1998

Batting Career:

M	I	NO	Runs	HS
198	325	36	13,165	210
Ave	**100**	**50**	**ct/st**	
45.55	29	68	106/16	

Bowling Career:

Runs	Wkts	Ave
2	0	-
BB	**5wi**	**10wm**
-	-	-

The declaration by the Essex captain, Doug Insole, was not on the face of it particularly generous; Northamptonshire were left to score 320 for victory in three and a quarter hours at Wellingborough School in August 1955, and the fact that they breezed home with plenty of time to spare was down to yet another sparkling innings – this time an unbeaten 172 – from their Australian left-hander, 'Jock' Livingston.

In almost any other era, the garrulous Sydneysider would have been a Test regular. Instead, he came to England as a Lancashire League professional and in 1948 was spotted by Jack Mercer on Northamptonshire's behalf as he hooked a fast bowler (in whom Mercer was also interested) to all parts of the ground. With the backing, almost inevitably, of British Timken, the County signed Livingston in the autumn of 1949, and he made his debut the following April.

His record for Northamptonshire bears the closest scrutiny. He passed 1,000 runs in seven of his eight seasons at Wantage Road, falling short only in 1952 when injury ruled him out

for half of the Championship programme. In both 1954 and 1955 he went past the 2,000 mark, and his career average of 45.55 for the County puts him second only to Allan Lamb among those players who have scored 5,000 runs. Team-mate Peter Arnold thought him to be 'probably the best left-hander in the country at the time.'

Livingston was also just the man to boost the County's recruiting efforts. His knowledge of the northern leagues paid handsome dividends as the likes of George Tribe, Keith Andrew and Frank Tyson were drawn into the fold. Tyson has described him as 'the Lord Kitchener of Northamptonshire.' It was a great blow when knee trouble forced Livingston to retire at the end of 1957, after which he retained his interest in the English game as a sales executive with Gray-Nicolls.

To the end of his life, Livingston harboured an admiration for Sir Donald Bradman which knew few if any bounds. That being so, the tribute paid by Bradman in the Livingston testimonial brochure of 1955 must have given its subject particular satisfaction: 'Jock himself is a student of the game, ever watchful, a true thinker and one of the many who have adorned this great game as a star adorns the night sky.'

Malachy Loye
RHB, 1991-

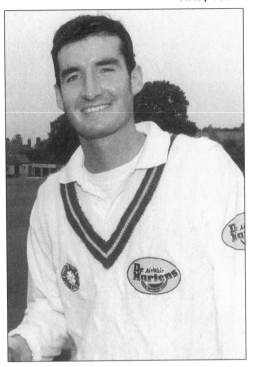

Born: Northampton, 27 September 1972				
Batting Career:				
M	**I**	**NO**	**Runs**	**HS**
113	180	17	5,797	322*
139	*134*	*15*	*3,565*	*122*
Ave	**100**	**50**	**ct/st**	
35.56	13	24	55	
29.96	*2*	*21*	*31*	
Bowling Career:				
Runs	**Wkts**	**Ave**		
43	0	-		
BB	**5wi**	**10wm**		
-	-	-		

It is possible to draw parallels between Mal Loye's career to date with Northamptonshire and *The Pilgrim's Progress*. There have been tantalising glimpses of the Delectable Mountains, notably in 1998 when he played the biggest and longest innings in the County's history. Yet within a year he was visiting the slough named Despond and encountering Giant Despair as a depressing loss of form cost him his first-team place.

Northampton-born of Irish parents – named after St Malachy, a twelfth-century archbishop of Armagh, and his biographer St Bernard – Loye played his early cricket in Cogenhoe, the village that was home to George Thompson a century earlier. He progressed through the County youth set-up and joined Northamptonshire's staff in 1990. Three years later, after coming close to 1,000 runs in his first full season, the Cricketers' Association voted him their Young Player of the Year, and he made his first England 'A' tour to South Africa.

A broken thumb, sustained while fielding in a benefit match the following summer, knocked him back. He struggled in 1995, regained his touch towards the end of 1996, then suffered a worrying back injury in 1997 which seemed to leave his future in some doubt. But he picked himself up again in 1998, and at the end of May he delighted a small County Ground crowd – Northampton Town's footballers were playing, and losing, at Wembley that day – by reaching 322 not out against Glamorgan, surpassing Northamptonshire's individual record of 300, which had been held since 1958 by Raman Subba Row. Loye batted for 649 minutes, faced 534 balls with 49 fours, and embarked upon a hot streak which brought him 981 Championship runs in nine innings.

The arrival of Bob Carter as Director of Cricket the following winter prompted him to sign a new long-term contract, and after the inexplicable horrors of 1999 this complex character offered an indication of his true ability in 2000, particularly during his match-winning 75 against a Worcestershire attack led by Glenn McGrath in the first floodlit National League game to be staged at the County Ground. Loye will hope that Mr Despondency grimly dogs his cricketing footsteps no more.

Neil Mallender

RHB and RFM, 1980-96

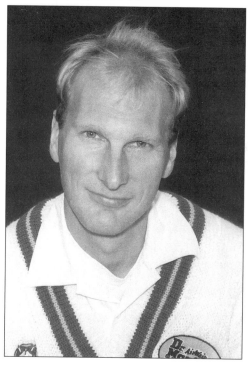

Born: Kirk Sandall, Yorks, 13 August 1961				
Batting Career:				
M	**I**	**NO**	**Runs**	**HS**
145	159	52	1,367	71*
134	*48*	*21*	*217*	*22*
Ave	**100**	**50**	**ct/st**	
12.77	-	2	47	
8.04	*-*	*-*	*28*	
Bowling Career:				
Runs	**Wkts**	**Ave**		
10,402	326	31.90		
4,041	*162*	*24.94*		
BB	**5wi**	**10wm**		
7-41	7	1		
7-37	*3*	*-*		

Neil Mallender's unusual career comprised nine seasons with Northamptonshire, in two spells, with eight years at Somerset inbetween. He finished with 937 wickets, also making one of the more remarkable England Test debuts in recent history, against Pakistan in 1992, and remains closely involved with the game as a first-class umpire.

The blond-haired fast bowler, soon dubbed 'Ghost' in the dressing room, seemed likely to prove the answer to Northamptonshire's prayers when he arrived at the County Ground in 1980, plucked from under the nose of Yorkshire. His immediate impact in Second XI cricket was, ironically, with the bat, but in 1981 he topped the side's Championship bowling averages and claimed 3-35 from 10 overs in the NatWest Trophy final against Derbyshire, a few days past his twentieth birthday.

At his best – fully fit, running in and pitching the ball up – Mallender could produce outstanding performances. He routed Derbyshire with 7-41 at the County Ground in 1982, and two years later took 7-37 against

Worcestershire in the second round of the NatWest, still a County record in the competition. Kapil Dev was a common denominator in these two efforts; team-mate in the first and a victim – clean bowled – in the second.

His decision not to seek a new deal with Northamptonshire at the end of 1986, partly on account of the lifeless home pitches, left the club 'deeply disappointed' according to the Annual Report, but Somerset were not complaining. He served them well, and at the age of thirty the England selectors called him up as a 'horses for courses' choice at Headingley. He captured eight Pakistani wickets in the game for 122, kept his place for the final Test at The Oval, and was promptly discarded. At least, as he observed afterwards, he had represented his country, something all professionals aspire to, but few achieve.

Mallender's return to Wantage Road in 1995 was not a great success, although no one could fault his commitment. Injuries restricted him to ten appearances in two seasons, and his contract was not renewed. He opted instead for the white coat and, after a summer on the reserve list, joined the main panel in 1999.

Jack Manning
LHB and SLA, 1954-60

Born: Adelaide, Australia, 11 June 1923
Died: Adelaide, Australia, 5 May 1988

Batting Career:

M	I	NO	Runs	HS
117	163	23	1,972	132
Ave	**100**	**50**	**ct/st**	
14.08	1	6	60	

Bowling Career:

Runs	Wkts	Ave
9,033	428	21.20
BB	**5wi**	**10wm**
8-43	24	4

Nicknamed 'Tanglefoot' or 'Tangles' for his idiosyncratic approach to the crease, Jack Manning joined forces with his fellow Australian slow left-armer, George Tribe, to give Northamptonshire a potent spin attack in the late 1950s. He played only four full summers of Championship cricket, but in three of them – 1956, 1957 and 1959 – he secured 100 wickets, before his County Ground career petered out in 1960.

Manning, whose bowling grip developed from his early baseball days in Adelaide, could make the ball buzz with fiercely-imparted spin, but after just three seasons with South Australia in the Sheffield Shield he came to England and, on the recommendation of Jock Livingston, Northamptonshire signed him in 1954. He spent his two qualifying seasons playing for Colne in the Lancashire League, and made an immediate mark on the Championship scene with 7-68 in only his second game, against a full-strength Surrey side at The Oval in May 1956.

Despite his success that year – 116 wickets at 20.68 – Manning approached the committee in mid-season to ask for his contract to be terminated. He was, he insisted, uncertain that his knee would stand up to the rigours of six days a week cricket, and also doubted his ability to make ends meet on what the club was paying him. By October, however, the request to be released had been withdrawn, and for the next three summers he continued to produce high-quality performances. Aside from his 104 wickets in 1957, he also scored 132 against Yorkshire at Harrogate, adding 191 with Keith Andrew. During the 1959 season he was as effective as ever with a career-best 8-43 against Gloucestershire at Peterborough.

Following the retirement of Tribe, Manning should have had an even more crucial role to play in 1960. Instead, the old knee trouble flared up again, and after a few disappointing games he found himself in the Second XI from late-July onwards. He tried again, after surgery, in 1961, but admitted that retirement was inevitable barring a 'miraculous' improvement. It didn't happen, and this engaging character returned to Adelaide where he played some club cricket, coached and became a publican.

T.E. 'Tim' Manning

RHB and WK, 1903-22

Born: Northampton, 2 September 1884
Died: Northampton, 22 November 1975
Batting Career:

M	I	NO	Runs	HS
53	93	15	1,026	57
(7	7	1	105	38)
Ave	**100**	**50**	**ct/st**	
13.15	-	3	29/3	
(17.50	-	-	2)	

Bowling Career:

Runs	Wkts	Ave
-	-	-
BB	**5wi**	**10wm**
-	-	-

'im' Manning was a cheerful and optimistic cricketer; a help, undoubtedly, when your team is dismissed for 27 and 15 in your first home match as Northamptonshire captain. As it was, that drubbing at the hands of Yorkshire in May 1908 did little to dampen the enthusiasm of the Old Wellingburian wicketkeeper, who had only been appointed skipper when the club's first choice, Lord Brackley (later the 4th Earl of Ellesmere), declined. Manning remained keenly interested in the club's affairs until his death at the age of ninety-one, serving on the committee for thirty years and holding the presidency from 1947 to 1956.

He made his debut in 1903, notching up 25 in a George Thompson-inspired success against Northumberland. After the tribulations of 1908 – the County using no fewer than thirty-one different players during the campaign – Manning offered his resignation, only to be talked into staying on. 'He has learned to take his defeats with a smile. Let us hope he is destined to smilingly

lead us to victory' said a supportive speaker at the Annual General Meeting in April 1909. And, after another dreadful start which saw seven of the first eight games lost, Manning began to do just that. Boosted by the arrival of Sydney Smith, Northamptonshire won eight out of nine games between mid-June and mid-August and moved up to seventh place in the Championship table.

Troubled by a back problem, Manning handed over the captaincy to 'Tubby' Vials at the end of 1910, only to find himself in the running for the job again nine years later. With no obvious contender to lead the side in the first post-war summer, Manning was approached. He was not prepared to take it on full-time, but held the fort until Joseph Noble Beasley had his arm twisted by a slightly desperate committee.

Manning also helped Northamptonshire out in 1922, skippering the opening game against Yorkshire after Captain Beattie, the mysterious army officer originally chosen to command the team, withdrew due to 'a domestic affliction.' It was Yorkshire again, and the County were routed by George Macaulay and Wilfred Rhodes for 81 and 42, losing at lunchtime on the second day. 'Tim' could still manage a smile.

Austin Matthews
RHB and RFM, 1927-36

Born: Penarth, 3 May 1904
Died: Llandudno, 29 July 1977
Batting Career:

M	I	NO	Runs	HS
224	369	44	5,127	116
Ave	**100**	**50**	**ct/st**	
15.77	2	14	109	

Bowling Career:

Runs	Wkts	Ave
14,999	567	26.45
BB	**5wi**	**10wm**
7-63	27	2

Northamptonshire had Austin Matthews' skill as a rugby union forward to thank for his arrival at Wantage Road. Welsh-born, he had joined Northampton RFC – 'The Saints' – and also turned out in club cricket in the area. He duly made his County debut in 1927 and qualified for Championship duty the following year, staying with the club for ten seasons and sustaining the seam attack through some difficult times, even by Northamptonshire standards.

'Matt' and his fellow Welshman, 'Taffy' Thomas, plugged away manfully through session after session, summer after summer. Statistically, his best performance for Northamptonshire was 7-63 in a losing cause against Worcestershire at Kettering in 1936. But the previous May, he and 'Nobby' Clark bowled the team to a famous victory at Taunton; Somerset were dismissed for 75 having needed only 124 to win, Matthews 5-31 and Clark 5-38. This became even more of a famous victory as the County had to wait four years for the next one!

Matthews could also score important runs down the order, and notched up a couple of centuries. In January 1937 he asked the committee for a testimonial, in recognition of his sterling service. They said he could have one in 1939, after Jack Timms.

Matthews had already accepted an offer to coach at Stowe School, and in July a letter arrived from Glamorgan, stating that Northamptonshire's long-serving opening bowler had approached his native county with a view to playing for them in August. His action was 'deprecated' by club officials, who nevertheless agreed that Matthews should be allowed to appear for Glamorgan 'without comment from this committee but also without our approval.'

The move worked wonders for Matthews who, within three weeks of his Glamorgan debut, was picked for England against New Zealand at The Oval. He turned amateur in 1946, upon his appointment as assistant-secretary, and retired the following year. *Wisden* for 1966 carried an article by him on the subject of coaching; some of the views expressed therein – 'I may be asked whether the game at the highest levels will decline if we do not coach all boys from a tender age. Not at all. There is not much chance that real genius will be overlooked' – might not find favour today.

Jack Mercer

RHB and RM, 1947

Born: Southwick, Sussex, 22 April 1893
Died: Westminster, London, 31 August 1987

Batting Career:

M	I	NO	Runs	HS
1 – Did not bat				

Bowling Career:

Runs	Wkts	Ave
100	2	50.00
BB	**5wi**	**10wm**
2-100	-	-

Jack Mercer is still remembered fondly at Wantage Road – for his sagacity, his enthusiasm and, above all perhaps, his humour. Although he played the bulk of his county cricket for Glamorgan, after a few games for his native Sussex, Mercer was an integral part of the Northamptonshire scene for thirty-six years. Keith Andrew remembers him as 'a wonderful cricketing tipster, a terrible horse-racing tipster and lovely man.'

His active career between the wars brought him more than 1,500 wickets with his seemingly endless variations, and when he answered Northamptonshire's advertisement for a coach in the winter of 1946/47, the club knew they were on to a good thing and appointed him following a single brief interview.

He made his solitary appearance for the County, in the midst of an injury crisis, against Hampshire in June 1947 at the age of fifty-two. 'Nobby' Clark, Reg Partridge and leg-spinner Bertie Clarke were all sidelined, so Mercer shared the new ball with Jack Timms. He sent down 26 overs, more than anyone else, and removed both Desmond Eagar, the Hampshire captain, and Leo Harrison. They were his last two Championship victims.

As a scout, he was shrewd and energetic; as a coach, extremely perceptive. Before Frank Tyson had even made his first-class debut, Mercer was warning the committee against 'burning out' their exciting new acquisition. Despite the occasional grouse from this or that local worthy that Mercer didn't spend enough of his Saturday afternoons looking for home-grown talent in the Northampton Town League, he remained on the coaching staff until 1963, when he transferred to the scorers' box.

There, he had more time and scope to demonstrate his conjuring tricks – he was a member of the Magic Circle – and indulge in another of his favourite pastimes, talking about cricket and cricketers. 'Everything's approximate!' was his scoring catchphrase, while at Eastbourne in 1980 he attributed his delayed arrival in the dressing room at the close of play to being 'weighed down by the bowling figures.' As Sussex had posted a total of 482-3 declared that day, he had a point.

Jack Mercer finally put down his pen in 1983, after two seasons recording the Second XI's doings, and died four years later. As David Foot has written: 'No one ever said a bad word about him.'

Born: Burnopfield, Co Durham,
23 October 1941
Died: Newton Aycliffe, Co Durham,
28 February 1990
Batting Career:

M	I	NO	Runs	HS
196	336	26	9,798	203
45	*42*	*2*	*610*	*84*
Ave	100	50	ct/st	
31.60	18	53	178	
15.25	*-*	*3*	*11*	

Bowling Career:

Runs	Wkts	Ave
2,559	83	30.83
936	*41*	*22.83*
BB	5wi	10wm
6-59	1	-
4-34	*-*	*-*

The Yorkshire-born, Kettering-based novelist and cricket fan, the late J.L. Carr, got it about right: 'Who remembers a year later, sometimes a month later, who won? It's the brilliant catch, the amazing run out, the strategical manoeuvre, the perfect stroke which are remembered.' He wrote that in 1961, just as Colin Milburn – a player who provided more of those special, lasting moments than most – was making his name with Northamptonshire. For so many County-watchers of the 1960s 'Ollie' remains, and will always remain, their favourite cricketer.

The arrival at Wantage Road of this 'well-built lad' (a classic *Wisden* euphemism) owed more to good fortune on the club's part than any grand design. Bill Coverdale, a Northamptonshire occasional from the 1930s, had settled in the north-east and recommended four Durham boys for a trial in 1959. Jack Mercer reckoned the seventeen-year-old Milburn 'could hit the ball' but nothing further was done until secretary Ken Turner, on holiday in Wales, heard that the youngster had notched a century for Durham against the Indian tourists. Hasty telephone calls revealed that Warwickshire were interested too. At length, Turner offered him an extra ten shillings a week, and Milburn joined Northamptonshire. It was, reckoned Turner, 'the best ten bob I ever spent.'

Milburn impressed in 1960, topping 1,000 runs for the Second XI to help them to the title, and duly established himself at first-class level with 1,334 runs in 1963, including hundreds against the West Indians and Yorkshire. Apart from his batting, which was always aggressive and exciting, he also shone at short-leg, where the quick reactions that enabled him to pull and hook so proficiently brought him a stack of catches – 43 in 1964, which is still a County record.

The following season, with Keith Andrew's team pressing for the Championship, Milburn struggled for runs until the final match, against Gloucestershire at Northampton. Victory was essential to keep alive the club's dwindling hopes, and the first day's play fell victim to the weather. Milburn's unbeaten 152 in three and a half hours, including 7 sixes and 15 fours, couldn't force the required result, but offered another thrilling glimpse of this rare talent.

His international career comprised just 9 Test matches, but he made a substantial

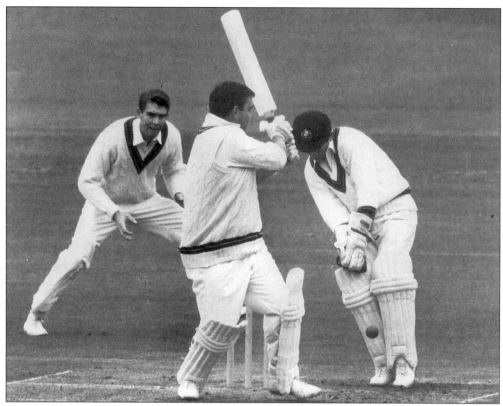

Colin Milburn hits out at a ball from John Gleeson, during Northamptonshire's first innings against Australia at Northampton, 25 May 1968. Milburn scored 90 before being caught by wicketkeeper Brian Taber, off Eric Freeman.

impact on four of them. Against the West Indies in 1966 he smashed 94 on debut at Old Trafford, and followed up with a match-saving 126 not out at Lord's, where the crowd's efforts to lift him shoulder-high were a tad optimistic. Two years later, on the same ground, he savaged Australia's attack for 83 on a rain-affected pitch, including a pull for six into the Grand Stand off Bob Cowper. The television footage of this knock ensures that future generations will be able to make their own assessment of his exhilarating strokeplay. A few months later, having blasted a memorable 243 for Western Australia against Queensland in Brisbane, he was called up to reinforce the MCC party in Pakistan, and contributed 139 in the final Test at Karachi.

There were welcome signs that the England selectors (whose decision to drop him later in the 1966 series had provided the motivation for his 203 before tea off the Essex bowlers at Clacton) might at long last be regarding Milburn as a decent long-term bet. But they never had the chance to pick him again. A car accident near Northampton in May 1969 cost him his left eye and, although he made a comeback in 1973 and 1974, augmenting his value to the side with some gentle seamers, his effective playing days were over.

Colin Milburn died at forty-eight, of a heart attack in a pub car park, after years of trying to find himself a settled niche in life. His passing left a great many people who had never met him, who knew his voice only as a radio commentator, who had never even seen him play at first-hand, feeling a keen sense of loss.

Vernon Murdin
RHB and RFM, 1913-27

Born: Wollaston, Northants,
16 August 1891
Died: Stonehouse, Gloucs, 11 April
1971
Batting Career:

M	I	NO	Runs	HS
171	278	69	1,767	90*
Ave	100	50	ct/st	
8.45	-	1	110	

Bowling Career:

Runs	Wkts	Ave
12,270	454	27.02
BB	5wi	10wm
8-81	28	4

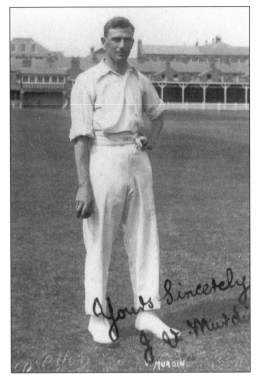

Another Wollaston yeoman, Vernon Murdin did plenty of bowling for Northamptonshire either side of the First World War. His out-swingers were particularly successful in the seasons immediately after the resumption of county cricket, but his career only extended to 1927, after which he accepted a coaching position at Wycliffe College.

Murdin made his debut in 1913, claiming Yorkshire's David Denton as a notable first victim, and against Kent at the County Ground in 1920 he performed Northamptonshire's first post-war hat-trick. When Warwick Armstrong's mighty Australians came to town the following summer, he gave his side the best possible start by bowling opener Edgar Mayne with the first ball of the match. Sadly, if predictably, it was all downhill from there; the tourists piled up 621 all out – Murdin taking 5-157 from 32.2 overs – and won with embarrassing ease by an innings and 484 runs. It remains the County's heaviest first-class defeat.

He recovered from that mauling to enjoy his best summer in 1922, capturing 91 Championship wickets including 8-81 against Glamorgan at Swansea and 7-44 in the home fixture with Kent – both match-winning efforts. 'Murdin stood out by himself among the bowlers who appeared all through the season' commented *Wisden*, and

in July he earned a place in the Players side against the Gentlemen at The Oval. He sat in the pavilion while Jack Hobbs, Phil Mead and the rest guided the professionals to 245-7, but rain prevented him from bowling a ball. Weather permitting, he would have shared the work with the illustrious Hampshire duo, Jack Newman and Alec Kennedy, with his County colleague 'Dick' Woolley in support.

His batting statistics are less than distinguished, although he remains in the record books by virtue of his last-wicket stand of 148 with Ben Bellamy against Glamorgan in 1925, his own contribution being 90 not out – the solitary half-century in 'Merry' Murdin's 278 knocks for the County. With the ball, he never recaptured his 1922 form on a consistent basis, and faded out in his mid-thirties. Although never granted a benefit, he was allowed a testimonial collection in 1928 – during the match against possibly his favourite opponents, Kent.

Mushtaq Mohammad
RHB and LB, 1965-77

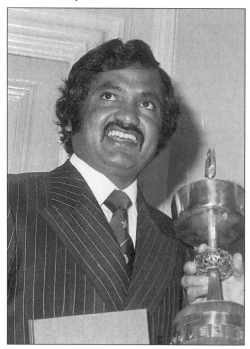

Born: Junagadh, India, 22 November 1943				
Batting Career:				
M	**I**	**NO**	**Runs**	**HS**
262	454	46	15,961	204*
162	*152*	*12*	*3,924*	*131*
Ave	**100**	**50**	**ct/st**	
39.12	32	89	175	
28.03	*1*	*19*	*41*	

Bowling Career:		
Runs	**Wkts**	**Ave**
13,224	551	24.00
1,265	*44*	*28.75*
BB	**5wi**	**10wm**
7-67	19	2
4-30	-	-

Mushtaq Mohammad captained Northamptonshire in 1976, the most successful season in the County's history. His side lifted the Gillette Cup at Lord's and finished as runners-up to Mike Brearley's Middlesex in the County Championship. Yet within a year, the brilliant Pakistani was a central figure in one of the most rancorous disputes the club has ever known – an upheaval which saw Mushtaq's distinguished career at Wantage Road come to an end in the unhappiest of circumstances.

One of four brothers to represent Pakistan – along with Hanif, Sadiq and Wazir – he was a first-class cricketer at thirteen years of age, and made his Test debut (the first of 57 appearances) at fifteen against the West Indies in 1959/60. Mushtaq toured England with the Pakistan team in 1962, returned the following summer as a member of the Pakistan Eaglets party (hitting a century at Peterborough), and during the latter trip he agreed a long-term contract with Northamptonshire to include his two-year qualification period. After the statutory couple of seasons sampling the delights of Corby, Lutterworth, Worksop and Crouch End with the Second XI, he stepped up to Championship cricket in 1966.

By the early 1970s he had fully come to terms with the disciplines and foibles of the county circuit. So many memories of that period revolve around Mushtaq and David Steele coming together with the scoreboard showing Northamptonshire not-many-for-two, and the pair going on to compile a big third-wicket partnership. His most prolific summer with the bat was 1972 when he notched 1,901 runs at 61.32, including 6 centuries, and also picked up 57 wickets with his leg-breaks and googlies. Even more special was his unbeaten 88, out of 210 all out, to set up the win over the Australians in August.

Mushtaq's elevation to the captaincy provided the denouement to a bizarre three-week drama at Wantage Road in 1975. Roy Virgin, the appointed skipper, stood down after the defeat against Middlesex on 29 July. Jim Watts replaced him for the next match, at home to Essex, but then broke a finger on the opening Saturday of the tour game against Australia. On Sunday 10 August, Steele assumed command for the Sunday League contest with Glamorgan at Wellingborough School, before heading off to join the England squad for the Third Test. So Mushtaq took the team down to Bournemouth

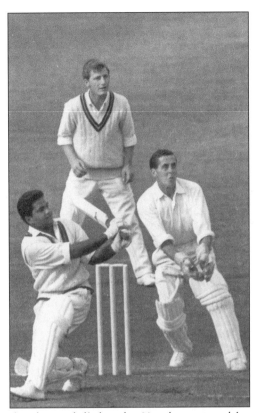

Mushtaq Mohammad's sparkling strokeplay delighted Northamptonshire followers in the 1960s and 1970s. Old differences set aside, he now coaches at the club's Centre of Excellence.

on 16 August, Hampshire were defeated inside two days, and the job was his.

His personal contribution in 1976 was substantial. In the Championship he averaged over 52, recording a County-best 204 not out to inflict more misery on Hampshire, and also netted his usual quota of important wickets. He didn't score particularly heavily in the Gillette Cup run but emerged at the end of it with Northamptonshire's first major trophy, notwithstanding the omission of Steele from the semi-final at Southampton and the decision to use Bishan Bedi to bowl the last over at Lord's; an over which cost 26 runs if not, happily, the match.

Even as the first of the champagne corks popped, secretary Ken Turner was planning for the future. The Northamptonshire team that was out there waving to the crowd had to

be rebuilt, he reasoned, and soon. But events were to overtake even the far-sighted Turner. The Kerry Packer story broke in May 1977 and Mushtaq was among the players to sign up with World Series Cricket. A succession of lengthy committee meetings in July and August culminated in the decision – taken while the '77 campaign was still in progress – to replace him with Watts as skipper for 1978. When word of this reached Mushtaq he not surprisingly resigned, angry and bitter, leaving initially Steele and then Geoff Cook to pick up the pieces for the last few games. There was to be no way back from there.

It is better by far to remember nimble-footed, sharp-eyed 'Mushy', the man credited with the invention of the reverse-sweep, as one of Northamptonshire's genuine star performers of the post-war era.

Robert Nelson
LHB and SLA, 1937-39

Born: Brook Green, London, 7 August 1912				
Died: Deal, Kent, 29 October 1940				
Batting Career:				
M	**I**	**NO**	**Runs**	**HS**
50	90	10	2,359	123*
Ave	**100**	**50**	**ct/st**	
29.48	2	16	20	

Bowling Career:		
Runs	**Wkts**	**Ave**
1,610	42	38.33
BB	**5wi**	**10wm**
3-7	-	-

A superficial examination of Robert Nelson's record as captain of Northamptonshire – two seasons, finishing bottom and next-to-bottom in the Championship table – might suggest a leader, not to mention a team, some way short of the required standard. In fact, he restored the County's cricketing pride, and offered welcome hope of better days to come. His tragically early death, in the Second World War at the age of twenty-eight, prevented him carrying through the rebuilding task he had begun so promisingly.

Nelson, a Cambridge blue with a few games for Middlesex behind him, arrived in Northamptonshire to take up a teaching post at Maidwell Hall in 1937. Officials at Wantage Road, desperately seeking a regular skipper, moved quickly, and in October of that year his appointment as captain for 1938 was confirmed. His inheritance was a dispirited side, without a victory since May 1935 and representing a club in dire financial straits. The improvement was anything but immediate – still nothing in the 'wins' column in '38 – but Nelson's own performances,

topping 1,000 runs with a century against Essex and 74 off Don Bradman's Australians, proved that Northamptonshire at last had a captain unquestionably worth his place as a player.

In May 1939, the drought was broken with a 78-run triumph over Nelson's old university at Fenner's. At the end of the month, Northamptonshire swamped Leicestershire by an innings and 193 runs at the County Ground, and they were underway again in the Championship. Nelson appeared on the pavilion balcony to address the large bank holiday crowd: 'I feel we have welded ourselves into a good side, and I do not think this should be our last victory' he said.

Only eighteen months later, Nelson was dead. A bomb dropped from an Italian aircraft exploded in front of the officers' mess at the Royal Marine depot in Deal, killing Nelson and a number of other servicemen. His passing prompted at least two poems (one of them by S.I. Philips who had played a handful of games with him for the County), and an elegant tribute by R.C. Robertson-Glasgow in *The Observer*: 'Here was optimism without credulity, tact without subservience, courage without obstinacy, kindness without indulgence.' Robert Nelson was indeed a leader worthy of the name.

Mick Norman
RHB, 1952-65

Born: Northampton, 19 January 1933
Batting Career:

M	I	NO	Runs	HS
202	364	17	10,165	152
7	7	-	*118*	*37**
Ave	**100**	**50**	**ct/st**	
29.29	15	50	99	
16.86	-	-	*2*	

Bowling Career:

Runs	Wkts	Ave	
76	2	38.00	
BB	**5wi**	**10wm**	
2-0	-	-	

Parochial types could always draw comfort from the sight of Mick Norman and Brian Reynolds – born in Northampton and Kettering respectively – going out to open the Northamptonshire innings. It took several seasons for Norman to establish himself in the first team, but having done so he scored heavily at the top of the order until his decision to forsake Wantage Road for Grace Road.

His first-class debut, against India in 1952, coincided with that of Frank Tyson, who regarded the young Norman as 'another Dennis Brookes in the making.' But only in 1959, Brookes' last season, did the fair-haired Northampton Grammar School old boy really make his presence felt with just over 1,000 runs and a maiden Championship century against Warwickshire. The following year, going in first regularly with Reynolds, Norman 'improved immensely' according to the Annual Report, and the four summers between 1960 and 1963 brought him 7,150 County runs.

He saved a good few more with his agile fielding in the covers. Indeed, Raman Subba Row pointed out to Norman that if he averaged 30 with the bat, but stopped 15 runs an innings in the field, he should think of himself as being 15 not out every time he took

guard. It was a clever piece of psychology on Subba Row's part which gave Norman's confidence a substantial and timely boost.

His 4 hundreds in 1963 included 152 against Nottinghamshire at Northampton, his highest for the County, but the next two seasons found him struggling for any degree of consistency. Against Glamorgan in 1964 he suffered the miserable experience of a 'king pair' – falling to the first ball of each innings, on the same day, to Ossie Wheatley both times. The match being at Swansea, it also meant a lot of steps to be descended and ascended again.

At the end of 1965, Norman made his move to Leicestershire and enjoyed a new lease of cricketing life. He played on until 1975, combining cricket with teaching in the last few years of his career, and adapted with conspicuous success to the rough-and-tumble of the John Player League which Leicestershire – helped by the forty-one-year-old Norman with his 'Sunday Nick' – won in 1974.

Albert Nutter

RHB and RFM, 1948-53

Born: Burnley, Lancs, 28 June 1913
Died: Cape Town, South Africa,
3 June 1996

Batting Career:

M	I	NO	Runs	HS
145	189	29	2,352	93
Ave	**100**	**50**	**ct/st**	
14.70	-	5	101	

Bowling Career:

Runs	Wkts	Ave
10,628	426	24.94
BB	**5wi**	**10wm**
7-52	21	2

Bert Nutter's most successful all-round season in county cricket was in 1938 when, as a Lancashire player, he scored 1,156 runs and claimed 91 wickets, just missing the 'double.' Ten years and a world war later he joined Northamptonshire, and thanks in no small measure to his beautifully smooth approach ('like running on a bed of air' commented one team-mate) with a bowling action to match, he maintained a high level of performance until he retired from the first-class game a few weeks after his fortieth birthday.

Nutter and his fellow Lancastrian, 'Buddy' Oldfield, were recruited in the winter of 1947/48, and both men quickly established themselves as County Ground favourites. Swinging the ball both ways, Nutter took 96 wickets for the County in his debut season and was the leading figure in a crushing victory over Kent by an innings and 200 runs, capturing 5-34 and 7-52 for a match return of 12-86. *Playfair Cricket Annual* reckoned him to be, in 1948, 'a better bowler than before the war.'

He was not as destructive the next year, and 1950 found him obliged to take on an extremely heavy workload – 885.2 overs in County matches, more than anyone else except the off-spinner Gordon Garlick. It was not surprising, perhaps, that his batting fell away, although he remained an outstanding slip fielder when he wasn't required for bowling. Northamptonshire were fortunate to have such a willing horse in their stable, for he sent down another 800 overs in 1951 with the reward of 86 wickets at 22 runs apiece. Playing much of his cricket on Northampton's flat, batsman-friendly pitches of the period – one of which was described by rival skippers Freddie Brown and Doug Insole of Essex, as 'quite useless' – this was a remarkable achievement.

Inevitably, the strain began to tell a little. Nutter got through his usual quota of overs in 1952, but then missed a third of the Championship programme the following season, which coincided with the testimonial fund for Oldfield and himself. He decided to call it a day, although his subsequent involvement in local cricket with the Horton House club ensured that Northamptonshire had not seen the last of him.

Born: Dukinfield, Cheshire, 5 May 1911
Died: Blackpool, 19 April 1996
Batting Career:

M	I	NO	Runs	HS
159	265	23	9,321	168
Ave	**100**	**50**	**ct/st**	
38.51	20	53	58	

Bowling Career:

Runs	Wkts	Ave
34	0	-
BB	**5wi**	**10wm**
-	-	-

At the tail end of the 1947 season, rumours began to circulate around the County Ground that an England player was on his way to Northamptonshire. It turned out to be the pint-sized Norman 'Buddy' Oldfield, a top-class strokeplayer whose first season with Lancashire in 1935 had been described in *Wisden* as 'sensational' and prompted Neville Cardus to observe: 'If this young man does not go to the top of his calling, there will be a scandalous interference with destiny.' In fact, he made 80 and 19 on his Test debut against the West Indies at The Oval, but the date was late August 1939; perhaps destiny had, after all, been interfered with, because he never played for his country again.

The British Timken connection smoothed Oldfield's path to Northampton in 1948. There were still a few details to be sorted out; he would, it was stressed, have to earn a Northamptonshire cap, although he was permitted to wear his England one in the meantime, and captain Arthur Childs-Clarke felt obliged to explain to anxious committee members that their new man 'had blinked all his life, and his nickname was "Blinkers".'

A nervous individual he may have appeared, with his blinking and chain-smoking (and his nerves were not helped, presumably, when a chimney pot crashed through the roof of his new home, narrowly missing his children), but Oldfield more than justified his salary, comfortably exceeding 1,000 runs in each of his six full seasons with the club and notching up 2,192 runs at 49.81 in 1949.

Oldfield and Bert Nutter were banned from Old Trafford, apart from when they visited as opponents, by the Lancashire authorities after both rejected their native county's post-war terms. 'Buddy' responded with delightful bloody-mindedness by scoring hundreds off the Lancashire attack in 1951, 1952 and 1953. But that last year found him troubled about his future; no longer, he complained, could he 'sight the ball accurately after 5pm.' Reluctant to lose his services, Northamptonshire offered him a new contract for 1954. In the event, he played three matches in May, hit 106 against Jim Laker, Tony Lock and the Bedsers, promptly retired and joined the first-class umpires list more or less at once.

Oldfield 'stood' in two Tests – one more than he had played in – and in 1968, old animosities resolved, he returned to Old Trafford as Lancashire's coach, staying in the job until 1972.

Reg Partridge
RHB and RFM, 1929-48

Born: Wollaston, Northants,
11 February 1912
Died: Northampton, 1 February 1997
Batting Career:

M	I	NO	Runs	HS
277	458	120	3,918	70
Ave	**100**	**50**	**ct/st**	
11.59	-	10	105	

Bowling Career:

Runs	Wkts	Ave
19,714	632	31.19
BB	**5wi**	**10wm**
9-66	22	2

In the spring of 1929, an enthusiastic seventeen-year-old took a day off from the boot factory where he worked to attend a trial at the County Ground. The youngster, Reg Partridge, had been recommended by Ben Bellamy, a fellow resident of Wollaston and the County's wicketkeeper. Unfortunately, no committee members turned up to see him; Partridge headed home again. And that might have been that, but for his determination to impress. He arranged another date, the officials made it this time, Partridge was duly taken on the staff and a few weeks later he opened his account of first-class wickets by nipping one back to bowl Herbert Sutcliffe at Bradford.

When this most loyal of professionals died, a few days short of his eighty-fifth birthday in 1997, he was Northamptonshire's last surviving Championship cricketer from the 1920s. A local hero throughout his long career, he was a talented enough bowler to hit the national headlines on occasions, most notably in 1938 when he dismissed Don Bradman cheaply at Wantage Road. This prompted The Western Brothers, Kenneth and George, to mention him in one of their then-famous topical songs: 'Partridge must feel such a cocky young bird/Bradman is out for two!'

He had claimed 9-66, bowling off-breaks rather than his usual medium-pace, against Warwickshire at Kettering in 1934, but gained rather more recognition for a 7-49 return at Blackpool five years later. Neville Cardus watched his beloved Lancashire struggle that day, and posed the question 'Why has nobody told me about Partridge?' in his *Manchester Guardian* piece, going on to compare the Northamptonshire man to Maurice Tate. It was a cutting to treasure – and treasured it was, to the end of his life.

Like so many others, Partridge lost potentially his best years to the Second World War. He played on afterwards, taking a hat-trick against Nottinghamshire at Trent Bridge in 1946, but back trouble prompted him to finish with first-class cricket at the end of 1948. He became groundsman at British Timken, living next to the company's sports field in Duston, and under his canny captaincy Timken dominated the Northants County League in its early seasons, winning the title no fewer than six times in the 1950s.

Tony Penberthy

LHB and RM, 1989-

Born: Troon, Cornwall, 1 September 1969				
Batting Career:				
M	**I**	**NO**	**Runs**	**HS**
148	218	24	5,268	128
196	*157*	*32*	*3,151*	*81**
Ave	**100**	**50**	**ct/st**	
27.15	5	30	88	
25.20	*-*	*16*	*51*	
Bowling Career:				
Runs	**Wkts**	**Ave**		
7,145	189	37.80		
5774	*195*	*29.61*		
BB	**5wi**	**10wm**		
5-37	4	-		
5-29	*4*	*-*		

The appointment of Tony Penberthy as Northamptonshire's vice-captain for 2001 recognised the considerable contribution made both on and off the field by the personable Cornishman over the previous few seasons. Always a useful performer in limited-overs cricket – adaptable with the bat, intelligent with the ball and a fine fielder – he also proved a pivotal member of the team that carried off the Championship's Division Two honours in 2000.

Penberthy, who first arrived at Northampton as a fourteen-year-old trialist, attracted national attention in 1989 when he claimed the wicket of Australian opener Mark Taylor with his opening delivery in first-class cricket. A photograph of this memorable moment hangs on the wall at Troon Cricket Club in Penberthy's home village, near Camborne. The following April he registered his maiden century, against Cambridge University at Fenner's, but the wait for a three-figure score in the Championship was to prove lengthy and often frustrating.

Uncertainty over his precise role in the longer game – front-line seamer who bats, or top-order batsman who bowls – hampered development, although 658 runs and 37 wickets earned him his Northamptonshire cap in 1994. Four years later, during an otherwise depressing summer for the side, he finally cemented a batting spot with two Championship hundreds – against Middlesex and Warwickshire – in as many months. He added another at Scarborough in 1999, a season which also yielded a National League hat-trick, only the second in the County's history, against Somerset at Northampton.

The 2000 campaign was a bitter-sweet affair for Penberthy. On the plus side he notched up 785 Championship runs, a figure exceeded only by Matthew Hayden, and he captained Northamptonshire to victory over Worcestershire in the first-ever floodlit National League fixture to be staged at Wantage Road. But the summer also saw the death of his father, Gerald, a well-known figure in Cornish sport who won a National Village Championship medal with Troon in 1973 and returned to Lord's eighteen years later to umpire the final between Harome and St Fagans. Penberthy junior, justly proud of his Cornish roots and of his father's achievements, was thus furnished with an added incentive to make a success of his new role.

91

Charles Pool
RHB, 1893-1910

Born: Northampton, 21 January 1876
Died: Epsom, Surrey, 13 October 1954
Batting Career:

M	I	NO	Runs	HS
94	177	6	4,350	166
(47	*70*	*1*	*1,659*	*157)*
Ave	**100**	**50**	**ct/st**	
25.43	4	20	51	
(24.04	*4*	*8*	*23/1)*	

Bowling Career:

Runs	Wkts	Ave
227	5	45.50
BB	**5wi**	**10wm**
4-53	-	-

Northamptonshire's team photographs from the early years of the last century usually feature a dashing figure in boater and cravat, moustache neatly trimmed, looking every inch the natty Edwardian. Charles James Tomlin Pool looked the part on the field too. 'There is no more delightful sight to our cricket loving crowds here in Northampton than watching the slim athletic form of Mr C.J.T. Pool at the wickets, gathering runs as easy as blackberries' wrote a contemporary reporter. Among his many aesthetically-pleasing knocks were Northamptonshire's maiden centuries in both the Second-Class Counties competition (157 against Durham in 1896) and the County Championship itself (110 off Hampshire's bowlers nine years later).

Pool was taught the rudiments of the game by his mother, and first appeared for the County side against Buckinghamshire at High Wycombe in the last fixture of 1893, aged seventeen. Supple of wrist, with a quick eye and a mercurial temperament, he played briefly for Little Lever in the Bolton League and was offered the secretaryship of a local building society as an incentive to stay there. Instead, he went to Australia for his health, declining an invitation to turn out for Archie MacLaren's 1901/02 touring side in an up-country match, and returned just in time to try his hand at first-class cricket with the County.

Charlie Pool was far and away the batting star in 1905, and the following year played his greatest innings for Northamptonshire. Against Worcestershire at New Road, the County followed on 165 behind with defeat looking certain; then Pool hit a brilliant 166 in three hours with 25 fours, and the home team, needing 254 to win, were bowled out by George Thompson for 212. This was cricket with a suitably Elgarian flourish, in the great composer's own native city. Northamptonshire's next Championship victory after following on was in 1988.

Pool often deputised as captain when the official appointee was absent, and was in charge when the County beat both Lancashire and Yorkshire for the first time. He retired in 1910 but didn't go too far away, coaching the club's young cricketers and running the County Hotel – now the County Tavern – until 1914. He was still scoring runs in club matches well into his fifties, and a bequest from his brother led to the erection of 'The Pool Gates' at the Wantage Road end of the ground in 1959.

Roger Prideaux

RHB, 1962-70

Born: Chelsea, London, 31 July 1939

Batting Career:

M	I	NO	Runs	HS
234	418	44	13,853	202*
46	*43*	*3*	*1,154*	*81*
Ave	**100**	**50**	**ct/st**	
37.04	24	73	142	
28.85	*-*	*9*	*17*	

Bowling Career:

Runs	Wkts	Ave
16	0	-
BB	**5wi**	**10wm**
-	-	-

The explosive Colin Milburn may have been Northamptonshire's brightest batting star in the 1960s, but Roger Prideaux's consistency was the perfect foil. The Cambridge blue passed 1,000 runs in each of his nine seasons at Wantage Road before heading for Sussex at the end of 1970, and his County average of just over 37 puts him in distinguished company.

Prideaux appeared for Kent in 1960 and 1961, but in September of the latter year secretary Ken Turner reported to Northamptonshire's committee that the twenty-two-year-old batsman was keen to move and make a long-term commitment to another club. He eventually signed on a special registration (contested by Kent) and in 1962, the final year of the distinction between amateur and professional in English cricket, he became Northamptonshire's 'assistant-secretary' and Keith Andrew's vice-captain. The succession had been established, and he duly took over from Andrew in 1967.

A strong driver of the ball, befitting a Tonbridge and Cambridge man, Prideaux scored the first of his 24 centuries for the County in only his second match, against Somerset at Peterborough in 1962. His form slipped three years later, when he skippered Northamptonshire to two of their thirteen victories in the chase for the Championship title, but he returned to his best in 1966 with 1,830 runs including a hundred in each innings at Trent Bridge. Prideaux was perfectly content to take the supporting role at Clacton in August as Milburn – intent on making a point to the erring England selectors – smashed 203 in an opening stand of 293!

Prideaux's own international career was even briefer than his partner's. He hit 64 in his debut innings against Australia at Headingley in 1968 but missed the final game of the series, at The Oval, through illness. Basil d'Oliveira took his place, made 158, and was chosen to tour South Africa – the rest is history. Prideaux went to Pakistan that winter and played in the Tests at Lahore and Dacca before, ironically, he was dropped in favour of Milburn.

After four summers as Northamptonshire's captain, Prideaux felt the need for a change. He remained with Sussex until 1973 and subsequently settled in South Africa, becoming a perceptive cricket commentator on radio and television.

Brian Reynolds

RHB and occ. WK, 1950-70

Born: Kettering, 10 June 1932
Batting Career:

M	I	NO	Runs	HS
426	732	65	18,640	169
36	*32*	*4*	*493*	*68**
Ave	**100**	**50**	**ct/st**	
27.94	21	95	299/20	
17.61	*-*	*1*	*15*	

Bowling Career:

Runs	Wkts	Ave
284	4	71.00
BB	**5wi**	**10wm**
1-0	-	-

As with Dennis Brookes, it is impossible to evaluate Brian Reynolds' contribution to Northamptonshire cricket solely in terms of his performances for the first team. They are impressive enough, but all the runs and catches, the 20 stumpings as stand-in wicketkeeper and – overlook these at your peril – the four wickets, must be supplemented with thirteen seasons' work as Chief Coach in charge of the Second XI, and a further eleven years in the specially-created role of Cricket Development Officer.

In John Arlott's words: 'In his own mind he is not only a cricketer, he is a Northamptonshire cricketer.' It is quite impossible to imagine the ever-loyal Reynolds following his agent's advice and moving to another county for a smarter car or a fatter wage packet; for that matter, it is equally impossible to imagine him employing an agent in the first place.

He joined the Northamptonshire staff in 1950 and made his Championship debut that summer – no qualification period was necessary for a Kettering boy, born and bred – against Sussex at Northampton. After national service,

and an opportunity to demonstrate his shoemaking skills at the Festival of Britain, he returned to the County Ground and broke through in 1956 by passing 1,000 runs for the first time to earn his County cap. Reynolds missed the entire 1959 season thanks to a football injury (he appeared for both Kettering Town and Peterborough United, later qualifying as a referee) but was hardly ever absent from the Northamptonshire side between 1960 and 1968, when he ceased to be an automatic choice.

Forming a reliable opening partnership with Mick Norman, Reynolds topped 1,500 runs in five consecutive summers. His best return was 1,843 in 1962, closely followed by 1,809 the year after. He also remained one of the fittest members of the staff, and his running between the wickets was being compared favourably with that of some of his younger colleagues as he moved into his mid-thirties. There was, in short, no more dedicated professional on the circuit.

It would have been the crowning glory of his benefit year, 1965, had Northamptonshire managed to win the Championship title. That they failed narrowly to do so was due in part to Worcestershire's victory over Hampshire at Bournemouth in a match of three declarations in late August. This caused, as *Wisden*

Brian Reynolds hooks a ball for 4 runs, during the first day of Middlesex v. Northamptonshire at Lord's in May 1963.

admitted, 'a great deal of controversy' and is still a talking point in the members' bar at Wantage Road to this day. Reynolds, the senior pro, had been playing golf with skipper Keith Andrew when the news came through of Colin Ingleby-Mackenzie's closure 146 runs behind; soon afterwards, Hampshire had been skittled for 31 to hand Don Kenyon's men the points. The ultimate disappointment of '65 notwithstanding, the triumvirate of Andrew, vice-captain Roger Prideaux and Reynolds still guided the club through some of the most successful seasons in its history.

The committee's decision to release him at the end of 1970 was less popular around the county than their appointment of him as coach three years later. Ken Turner knew his man: 'I want you to get these lads (in the Second XI) so tired during the day that they won't have any energy left to go out at night!' Reynolds did indeed work young

professionals hard. Those who were serious about wanting first-team cricket, like David Capel and Rob Bailey, got on with it and duly achieved their goal; others less diligent fell by the wayside.

Later, as one of the first CDOs in the country, he spread the cricketing gospel into Northamptonshire schools and developed the Centre of Excellence scheme which has thrown up a number of talented youngsters over the last decade. He also travelled many miles each summer on scouting missions, never without deckchair, binoculars, flask of tea and copy of the *Daily Telegraph*. When Brian Reynolds officially retired in 1997, chairman Lynn Wilson spoke nothing more than the truth in that year's Annual Report: 'Throughout the long history of the County Cricket Club there have been few, if any, individuals more committed and dedicated to Northamptonshire's cause.'

David Ripley
RHB and WK, 1984-

Born: Leeds, 13 September 1966
Batting Career:

M	I	NO	Runs	HS
291	384	98	8,200	209
257	*158*	*65*	*1,633*	*52**
Ave	**100**	**50**	**ct/st**	
28.67	9	32	628/81	
17.56	*-*	*1*	*213/29*	

Bowling Career:

Runs	Wkts	Ave
103	2	51.50
BB	**5wi**	**10wm**
2-89	-	-

When the almost laughably boyish David Ripley walked out as 'nightwatchman opener' against the West Indies at Bletchley in 1984, it was tempting to ask if his folks knew he was out so late. He showed his mettle then, defying Malcolm Marshall, Courtney Walsh, Eldine Baptiste and the rest to make a brave 42, and has done so many times since, both with the bat and behind the stumps. A fresh and substantial challenge came along in the shape of the Northamptonshire captaincy for 2001 – making him the first wicketkeeper officially appointed to the job since Keith Andrew.

The young Yorkshireman was handed the gloves in the summer of '84 when the long-time incumbent, George Sharp, broke a thumb against Warwickshire in late June. Ripley had, in fact, already pulled off two 'unattributed' stumpings in the Championship as a substitute in 1983; an occurrence no longer permissible under Law 2. Another injury to Sharp in 1985, and his subsequent retirement, seemed to leave the way clear for the nineteen-year-old, until Northamptonshire provided competition in the shape of the former Kent 'keeper Stuart

Waterton. They shared the duties in 1986, but Ripley produced a trump card in the penultimate fixture, at Scarborough, when he hit a match-saving 134 not out against his native county. Since then, apart from during 1995 when Allan Lamb preferred Russell Warren in the interests of team balance, he has been the club's number one gloveman, always giving of his best.

Ripley enjoyed his most productive season in 1988, claiming 81 dismissals and fulfilling a lifetime's ambition when 'caught Ripley, bowled Lillee' appeared in the scorebook for the first time, courtesy of a nick by Hampshire's Kevan James at Bournemouth. Ten years later, he enjoyed his finest achievement with the bat to date, making 209 in a fifth-wicket stand of 401 with Mal Loye, which created a new English first-class record.

He impressed as skipper in 1999 when, deputising for Matthew Hayden, he led Northamptonshire to three of their four Championship wins. He was, according to Director of Cricket Bob Carter, 'the natural choice' to succeed Hayden for 2001. For Ripley himself, having attained the hard-won status of Northamptonian-by-adoption, it was simply 'a great honour.'

David Sales

RHB, 1996-

Born: Carshalton, Surrey, 3 December 1977

Batting Career:

M	I	NO	Runs	HS
62	97	7	3,150	303*
78	*74*	*12*	*1,769*	*84**
Ave	**100**	**50**	**ct/st**	
35.00	6	14	42	
28.53	*-*	*11*	*28*	

Bowling Career:

Runs	Wkts	Ave
163	9	18.11
30	*0*	*-*
BB	**5wi**	**10wm**
4-25	-	-
-	*-*	*-*

When Brian Reynolds, a vastly experienced judge of talent not given to indulging in wild hyperbole, returned from an English Schools Cricket Association Under-15s festival at Lincoln describing a young batsman there as the best he had seen since Peter May, Northamptonshire officials would have been foolish to ignore him. Thanks largely to Reynolds' efforts, David Sales – a Surrey boy – opted for Wantage Road, and has already written his name prominently in the record books with power to add.

He made the first of those entries on 18 September 1994, at the end of his first season on the staff, with an unbeaten 70 off 56 balls in the Sunday League game against Essex at Chelmsford. Aged 16 years 289 days, he was the youngest player to score a half-century in the competition. Two years later, at Kidderminster, Sales had the number-crunchers in a rare old tizzy when he notched 210 not out (after a duck in the first innings) on his first-class debut against Worcestershire. It was the first double-century by a debutant in a Championship match, and among Englishman only W.G. Grace, 130 years before, had reached 200 at an earlier age. Follow that, as they say.

The burden of expectation proved heavy over the next couple of years, but in 1999 he rediscovered his appetite for runs with 303 not out against Essex at Northampton. There was, inevitably, a record attached: the youngest English triple-centurion, at 21 years 240 days. Mal Loye's unbeaten 322 stood in Sales' sights until last man Michael Davies was run out, much to his partner's disgust! Further big innings – 205 later that season against Leicestershire, and 276 off the Nottinghamshire attack in 2000 – gave him four double-hundreds or better for Northamptonshire, a tally exceeded only by Dennis Brookes. Coincidentally, Brookes also registered his first 'double' at Kidderminster, half a century before Sales in 1946.

Leaving aside all the facts and figures, 'Jumble' has proved himself an exciting player to watch; powerful and combative, with natural timing to delight everyone except the bowler on the receiving end. Sadly, a serious knee injury sustained in Grenada on New Year's Day 2001 put on hold Sales' bid for Test recognition. At least he has time on his side.

Sarfraz Nawaz

RHB and RFM, 1969-82

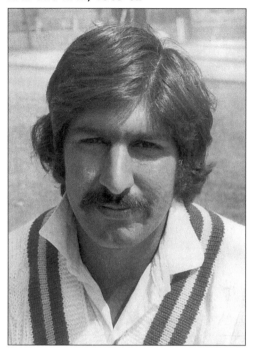

Born: Lahore, Pakistan, 1 December 1948

Batting Career:

M	I	NO	Runs	HS
151	198	44	3,212	90
160	*113*	*40*	*1,177*	*59**

Ave	100	50	ct/st
20.85	-	10	88
16.12	*-*	*2*	*26*

Bowling Career:

Runs	Wkts	Ave
11,962	511	23.40
4,587	*224*	*20.48*

BB	5wi	10wm
7-37	24	-
5-15	*3*	*-*

Sarfraz Nawaz and controversy were inextricably entwined for many years, both during and after his playing career. But the Pakistani enjoyed some excellent seasons with Northamptonshire, especially during his second spell at Wantage Road, and claimed more than half of his first-class wickets – 511 out of 1,005 – in the County's cause.

Early in 1969 the club received a letter from the captain, Roger Prideaux, who was touring Pakistan with Colin Cowdrey's MCC team. Sarfraz, then twenty years old, made his Test debut in the final game of the series in Karachi, and Prideaux reported that the young paceman was looking to come to England with a view to qualifying for Championship cricket in 1970. Northamptonshire took him on, and his first appearance was in the 65-run victory over the West Indies in May; Colin Milburn's last match before his car accident. 'Saf' fared well enough the following summer with 59 wickets, but had a dismal time of it in 1971 when his tour of England with Pakistan was ruined by a back problem. A handful of late-season games for the County then did him no favours, and he was released at the end of the year.

In 1974, the summer of Pakistan's next visit, he returned to Northamptonshire. The two intervening seasons had brought him runs and wickets aplenty as Nelson's professional in the Lancashire League, and he put the experience gained there to excellent use for both the County and his country. He took 98 wickets at 20.29 for Northamptonshire in 1975, troubling batsmen around the circuit with extra pace and late movement, and followed up with 82 wickets in 1976, also helping Mushtaq's side secure the Gillette Cup. He led the club's averages again in 1977 with 73 wickets at 17 runs apiece.

Sarfraz's performances during the 1980 Benson & Hedges Cup campaign marked the summit of his achievements with the County. In the last three rounds, culminating in the narrow Monday triumph over Essex at Lord's, he posted aggregate figures of 11 wickets for 66 runs in 31 overs. An injury-hit season in 1981, and the signing of Kapil Dev, led to his second and final departure from Northampton at the end of 1982, although the future politician's frequently stormy Test career stretched into 1984.

Malcolm Scott

RHB and SLA, 1959-69

Born: Westoe, Co Durham, 8 May 1936				
Batting Career:				
M	**I**	**NO**	**Runs**	**HS**
183	249	63	2,426	62
11	*6*	*2*	*44*	*19**
Ave	**100**	**50**	**ct/st**	
13.04	-	1	90	
11.00	*-*	*-*	*6*	
Bowling Career:				
Runs	**Wkts**	**Ave**		
11,208	457	24.52		
263	*19*	*13.84*		
BB	**5wi**	**10wm**		
7-32	20	4		
3-6	*-*	*-*		

The departure of George Tribe and Jack Manning, together with Mick Allen's loss of form, opened the way for Malcolm Scott, a left-arm spinner from Durham, to show what he could do in first-class cricket. Scott, also a talented footballer, had taken up residence in Northampton in 1957, and after national service he turned out against India and Cambridge University in 1959.

As is so often the case in county cricket, it took one player's misfortune to bring another to the fore. Allen, the third member of Northamptonshire's formidable trio of slow left-armers in the late 1950s, began the 1961 season well enough, but then 'lost his length and direction in a most disappointing manner' according to the Annual Report. Scott was the immediate beneficiary. With Allen in the Second XI by the end of July, Scott saw out the summer and finished with 69 wickets at 22.72, second only to David Larter in the County averages. However, it was all change again in 1962; Scott struggled, Allen was back at his best, and the Bedford man took his turn to claim runners-up spot to Larter in the final statistics.

It was only in 1964, following Allen's move to Derbyshire, that Scott finally secured his first-team berth. He played in all 30 matches and captured 113 wickets – including a career-best 7-32 against Sussex at Hastings – at 19.27 each. No one has managed a bigger haul for the County in the thirty-six seasons since then. He proved effective again in the 1965 Championship bid, sending down more overs than anyone except Brian Crump, and accounting for 67 batsmen. He and Crump skittled Essex for 88 at Clacton to snatch victory in a game of three declarations. But the next summer found him troubled by injury, and his career ran into serious trouble in 1967 when the legality of his bowling action was called into question. The MCC banned Scott for the last two games of the year.

Not surprisingly, perhaps, he failed to make much of an impact thereafter. By 1969, Northamptonshire were entertaining high hopes of a young left-arm spinner from Staffordshire, Dennis Breakwell. It spelt the end of Malcolm Scott's time at the County Ground, made memorable by the transient triumphs of 1964 and 1965.

George Sharp
RHB and WK, 1968-85

Born: West Hartlepool, Co Durham, 12 March 1950

Batting Career:

M	I	NO	Runs	HS
305	395	80	6,243	98
285	*203*	*52*	*2,377*	*51**
Ave	**100**	**50**	**ct/st**	
19.81	-	21	564/90	
15.74	*-*	*1*	*242/50*	

Bowling Career:

Runs	Wkts	Ave
70	1	70.00
BB	**5wi**	**10wm**
1-47	-	-

George Sharp's praiseworthy career with Northamptonshire forges an historically-satisfying link between two of the County's other long-serving wicketkeepers. He joined the staff in 1966, Keith Andrew's final year in the first-class game, and was succeeded on his retirement by David Ripley. This was a formidable dynasty, comprising the top three stumpers in the club's all-time dismissals list with well over 2,000 victims between them.

Sharp was signed on as a sixteen-year-old from West Hartlepool, and sampled first-team cricket against Cambridge University a couple of seasons later. After impressing in the final six Championship matches of 1970, not least with some useful runs in the lower order, Sharp got the nod ahead of Laurie Johnson at the start of 1971. A broken finger in late June proved merely a temporary setback for him; he regained his status as first-choice 'keeper in 1972 and was to retain it through some of Northamptonshire's most successful times.

The club's active recruitment policy in the 1970s threw up a series of new challenges for Sharp; he kept efficiently to the pace of Sarfraz, Cottam and Dye, and relished the subtle, slow left-arm variations of Bishan Bedi. He also continued to make telling contributions with the bat, something Johnson had rarely managed to do, although a first-class century eluded him. He came closest against Yorkshire at Northampton in 1983, perishing two runs short after dragging the side out of trouble with characteristic determination.

In limited-overs cricket he encouraged quietly, kept a cool head when it mattered, and – as in the longer game – provided valuable back-up to an increasingly formidable batting unit. He also proved himself a capable leader in Geoff Cook's absence.

Two nasty breaks, a thumb and a finger, precipitated the end of his playing career in 1985. He may have been less spectacular and 'showy' than some of his contemporaries, but there was considerable respect around the circuit for a consummate professional who got on with the job. Keen to stay in cricket, he joined the first-class umpires list in 1992, and officiated in his first Test match – England against India at Trent Bridge – four years later. He now travels the world as a member of the international panel.

Born: Daventry, 10 July 1859				
Died: Northampton, 29 November 1942				
Batting Career:				
M	**I**	**NO**	**Runs**	**HS**
31	55	25	393	38*
(110	*137*	*37*	*2,049*	*139*)*
Ave	**100**	**50**	**ct/st**	
13.10	-	-	43/4	
(20.49	*2*	*6*	*147/37)*	

Bowling Career:

Runs	Wkts	Ave
-	-	-
BB	**5wi**	**10wm**
-	-	-

There was no talk of 'shamateurism' with Charlie Smith, Northamptonshire's regular wicketkeeper for sixteen years including the first two seasons in the County Championship. A shoe riveter, he regularly put in a few hours' work at his last before heading to the County Ground for a half past eleven or midday start. It was a pity that first-class status only came when Smith, a great stalwart, was well past his best behind the stumps.

Smith turned out for the Temperance club in the early years of Northampton Town League, and 1887 saw him earn a late call-up into the County side against Hertfordshire at St Albans; so late, in fact, that he was 'absent' in the first innings – a problem with the stitching, perhaps? But he claimed three catches, and after a sprinkling of matches over the next three years, Smith made the gloves his own in 1891. James Lillywhite's *Cricketers' Annual* does not go overboard on technical analysis of the Northamptonshire newcomer: 'Good wicketkeeper, hard-hitting bat.'

He scored runs occasionally, in a style described by Jim Coldham as 'hectic.' His only two centuries for the County were made in successive games during July 1897; an unbeaten 139 against Uppingham Rovers and, rather more commendably, 103 off a respectable Nottinghamshire attack at Trent Bridge. He actually headed the batting averages in 1900, but his effectiveness subsequently declined markedly. By 1904, Northamptonshire's final campaign in the Second-Class Counties competition, Smith was down at number eleven.

The club's promotion in 1905, when he was nearly forty-six, afforded Smith plenty of opportunity to add some illustrious autographs to his collection. He asked notable opponents to sign a bat that had once belonged to Tom Plumb, one of his predecessors as Northamptonshire stumper and rated alongside England's other two wicketkeeping Ps – Ted Pooley and George Pinder – during the 1860s and 1870s.

Although the spirit was still willing, Smith retired in 1906 and served briefly as a first-class umpire. Part of the proceeds of a 'Country Fair' at the County Ground in 1907 were presented to him as a well-deserved testimonial, and he later joined the club's committee. Even in the 1930s, players would buy their boots and shoes from him: 'You can pay me next week' became something of a catchphrase.

Sydney Smith

LHB and SLA, 1907-14

Born: San Fernando, Trinidad,
15 January 1881
Died: Auckland, New Zealand,
25 October 1963
Batting Career:

M	I	NO	Runs	HS
119	210	13	6,396	204
Ave	**100**	**50**	**ct/st**	
32.46	12	31	87	

Bowling Career:

Runs	Wkts	Ave
8,744	502	17.41
BB	**5wi**	**10wm**
8-39	36	8

There is nothing unusual these days about counties snapping up West Indian cricketers to bolster their squads. It was rather less common in 1906 when Sydney Gordon Smith, a white Trinidadian with a Scottish father and English mother, was approached by Northamptonshire officials anxious to make their newly-promoted team more competitive at first-class level. They had been able to gauge Smith's abilities at first hand; he had bowled the West Indians to victory at the County Ground that year with a match haul of 12-99. George Thompson had also spoken highly of him following Lord Brackley's tour to the Caribbean in 1904/05, and history was to prove Thompson a sound judge.

Smith, a cultured left-handed batsman as well as an outstanding left-arm spinner, decided to leave his desk at the Government Works Department in Port-of-Spain and start to qualify for Northamptonshire. He might have wondered what he was letting himself in for during the English summer of 1907, which he spent shivering in the dressing room with cold and the after-effects of malaria when he wasn't turning out for Northamptonshire Club and Ground against various local amateur sides. But having acclimatized he wasted no time making his mark in the Championship.

In 1909, his first full season, he logged 833 runs and 94 wickets in the 18 games, and Lord Hawke was said to be considering whether Smith might 'become' English for Test match purposes. He topped 1,000 runs the following year, including 204 against Gloucestershire at Wantage Road, and shared the limelight with Thompson in the County's stunning 1912 title challenge. Succeeding 'Tubby' Vials as captain during 1913, Smith found the responsibility invigorating and duly became the first cricketer to do the 'double' for Northamptonshire – 1,424 runs, with 4 centuries, and 107 wickets. In 1914 he dismissed four batsmen in four balls against Warwickshire at Edgbaston, the first three all being caught by Thompson at slip.

Northamptonshire paid Smith to do clerical work for the club during the winter, but on the outbreak of war they released him to enable him to take a job with the Capital & Counties Bank. In 1915 he went to New Zealand – 'without communicating his intentions' according to the club's minutes – and chose to stay there, appearing for Auckland until 1925/26. Their gain was, all too obviously, Northamptonshire's loss.

Born: Peterborough, 15 August 1913
Died: Peterborough, 7 May 1981
Batting Career:

M	I	NO	Runs	HS
136	250	10	4,343	128
Ave	**100**	**50**	**ct/st**	
18.09	2	20	46	

Bowling Career:

Runs	Wkts	Ave
22	2	11.00
BB	**5wi**	**10wm**
1-5	-	-

To Alex Snowden of Peterborough fell the honour, in 1934, of scoring the first century for Northamptonshire against the Australians. As he put it many years later: 'Every dog has his day. This was mine.' He managed only one other three-figure score, but nevertheless did his bit to keep the County's flag flying during the grim 1930s.

His early cricketing education was at King's School in his native city, supplemented by coaching from Aubrey Faulkner and Andrew Sandham. His father, Alderman William Snowden, was a prominent citizen of Peterborough, and was on hand at the Crawthorne Road ground in July 1932 when skipper 'Beau' Brown presented the eighteen-year-old Alex with his County cap. The teenager captained Northamptonshire himself that season, against Gloucestershire at Bristol, and a battling half-century off the touring Indians at Kettering seemed to further justify the club's hopes that it had a genuine home-grown amateur talent on its hands.

Snowden's 'day' came a couple of years later when the men from Down Under, including Don Bradman, visited Wantage Road. The Australians totalled 284 and Snowden, who opened with Fred Bakewell, then held Northamptonshire's reply together; the next highest scorer was Jack Timms with 27.

Snowden got to 97, with Reg Partridge at the other end, and a high full-toss from 'Chuck' Fleetwood-Smith was pulled gratefully to the boundary to secure his place in history. Bradman and Bill O'Reilly were quick to congratulate him, 'Tiger' dismissing him moments later for 105. That summer also saw him share two century opening partnerships with Fred Bakewell against Warwickshire – on the same day!

Snowden continued to lead the team on occasions – including the match at Bradford in 1934 which featured Dennis Brookes' first-class debut – and took over for the first part of the 1935 season when Brown was injured. But Snowden's batting form deserted him, and there is a hint of some behind the scenes aggravation; in July the club's president, Stephen Schilizzi, went to see Alderman Snowden with the intention, according to the committee minutes, of 'easing the unpleasant situation.' His diplomacy must have worked, for Alex continued to play for the County, as often as business commitments allowed, until 1939.

David Steele

RHB and SLA, 1963-84

Born: Bradeley, Staffs, 29 September 1941

Batting Career:

M	I	NO	Runs	HS
416	673	101	18,231	140*
194	*170*	*28*	*3,317*	*109*
Ave	**100**	**50**	**ct/st**	
31.87	25	92	469	
23.36	*1*	*16*	*64*	

Bowling Career:

Runs	Wkts	Ave
11,533	462	24.96
1,389	*40*	*34.72*
BB	**5wi**	**10wm**
8-29	16	2
4-35	*-*	*-*

A good few Northamptonshire people have only once voted for the winner of the BBC's 'Sports Personality of the Year' poll. That was in 1975, when David Steele took home the famous television camera trophy by virtue of his sterling performances in that summer's Test series against Australia. For so long the archetypal English county professional, Steele became national property – a national treasure, indeed – for two summers, before the authorities dropped him like a stone.

'Stan' heard of his selection for the Lord's Test of '75, called up for the first time at thirty-three to bolster England's fragile batting, while travelling up the M1 to Dudley for a Sunday League game against Worcestershire. Jim Watts had bet Steele a fiver that he would be in the team, and the grey-haired, bespectacled warrior from Staffordshire – in his benefit year, to boot – was photographed paying up.

A few days later he embarked on his own Churchillian walk with destiny, by way of the downstairs toilets at 'Headquarters' following one of cricket history's best-known wrong turnings, and confronted the menace of Dennis Lillee and Jeff Thomson in a manner that inspired the whole country, not least the Fourth Estate. Clive Taylor's description – 'The Bank Clerk Goes To War' – is perhaps best-remembered, while Frank Keating pinpointed Steele's wider appeal, specifically 'his legion of supporters which included by then a considerable lobby of housewives who couldn't tell lbw from PVC.'

His scores from that series should be engraved on the heart of every true Northamptonian: 50 and 45 at Lord's, 73 and 92 at Headingley, 39 and 66 at The Oval. He led off the following summer with 106 in the opening Test against the West Indies at Trent Bridge, and fared better than most in the remainder of the series, which England lost comfortably. And then he was discarded. Wouldn't be able to handle the spinners in India, they said. The selectors were not, presumably, present on the County Ground in July 1975 when Steele made 84 out of 138 all out against Derek Underwood on a worn pitch – 'masterly' according to *Wisden*.

The cousin of Brian Crump and brother of John Steele, a Leicestershire stalwart who joined the first-class umpires list in 1997, David made his Northamptonshire debut in 1963 and quickly established his reputation as a reliable performer, notching runs in the middle-order and picking up handy wickets with his left-arm spin. As Brian Reynolds

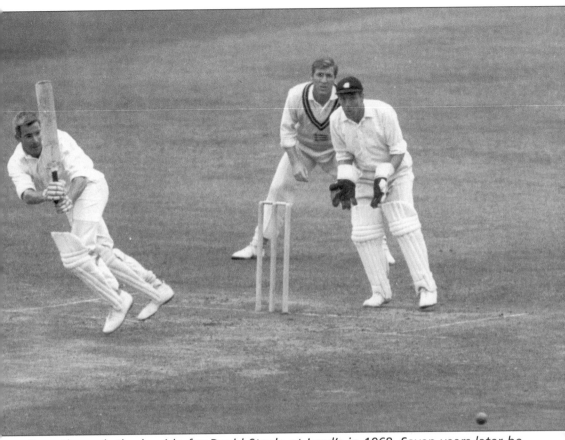

Runs through the legside for David Steele at Lord's in 1968. Seven years later he became an English sporting hero after successfully confronting Dennis Lillee and Jeff Thomson.

recalls: 'If the ball went past his eyebrows, he pulled down his cap and got on with it. I wish we had a few more like him.' Steele reached 1,000 runs for the County in nine seasons, proving especially prolific from 1971 onwards. He and Mushtaq Mohammad carried the batting to a large extent during Jim Watts' first stint as captain which saw Northamptonshire secure three successive top four finishes in the Championship.

His England heroics over, and the deep freezer full of meat courtesy of a local butcher who sponsored him at one lamb chop a run against Australia, Steele opted for a change of scenery and joined Derbyshire as skipper in 1979. The move came as a surprise to most as he had already turned down the captaincy of Northamptonshire, and his reign at Derby lasted barely half a season. He returned to Wantage Road in 1982 and made a major impact with the ball, claiming nearly 200 wickets in three summers before an arthritic condition in his hip forced him to retire in 1984.

Having given Northamptonshire excellent service with bat, ball and in the field (as a superb close-catcher, particularly at backward short-leg), he maintained his involvement as a committee member and returned to his original trade as a printer. Still in demand as an after-dinner speaker, he is always happy to regale an audience with anecdotes from his days as England's unlikely sporting hero; days when, in his own words, 'you wanted to try until it hurt.'

Raman Subba Row

LHB and occ. LB, 1955-61

Born: Streatham, London, 29 January 1932				
Batting Career:				
M	**I**	**NO**	**Runs**	**HS**
113	186	25	7,050	300
Ave	**100**	**50**	**ct/st**	
43.78	19	28	80	
Bowling Career:				
Runs	**Wkts**	**Ave**		
721	23	31.34		
BB	**5wi**	**10wm**		
3-22	-	-		

Raman Subba Row retired from first-class cricket at the age of twenty-nine, following a season which had seen him notch two Ashes centuries against Australia. Figures may never tell the whole story, but a career record of more than 14,000 runs at 41.46 (and he averaged nearly 47 in his 13 Tests) indicates a batsman with a healthy appetite for getting in and building a score; he surely had plenty of hundreds left in him when the claims of business prevailed.

Subba Row went from Cambridge University to Surrey, who were just beginning their lengthy domination of the county scene. At the end of 1954, Northamptonshire were granted permission to sound him out about a move to Wantage Road. Within three months of his debut he had set a new mark for the highest individual score ever made for Northamptonshire – 260 not out in seven and three-quarter hours against Lancashire at the County Ground.

After two years in the RAF he prepared to resume his County career in 1958,

having been appointed captain in place of Dennis Brookes, who had led the side to second place in the Championship in 1957. It was a messy business which reflected little credit on the committee but a great deal on Brookes and Subba Row, who got on with it and helped Northamptonshire to fourth spot in 1958. In May of that year, the new skipper broke his own record with 300 against his old county at The Oval, made in nine and a half hours with 42 fours. It was testimony to what Frank Tyson described as his 'monolithic concentration and unshakable determination.' He may not have possessed all the strokes, but used the ones that were in his repertoire to maximum effect.

Subba Row continued to mix Test and Championship cricket until 1961 when, with his amateur status the subject of enquiries from Lord's, he decided to retire. He later served as chairman of both Surrey and, between 1985 and 1990, the Test and County Cricket Board. He was among the first to congratulate – by fax – Mal Loye on beating his forty-year-old individual record in 1998, advising Loye to watch out for another would-be record-breaker in 2038!

Haydn Sully

LHB and OB, 1964-69

Born: Sampford Brett, Somerset,
1 November 1939

Batting Career:

M	I	NO	Runs	HS
110	123	46	624	48

1 – Did not bat

Ave	100	50	ct/st
8.10	-	-	58

Bowling Career:

Runs	Wkts	Ave
8,129	302	26.91
39	*2*	*19.50*

BB	5wi	10wm
7-29	15	2
2-39	*-*	*-*

Off-spinner Haydn Sully enjoyed one outstanding season with Northamptonshire after being recruited from his native Somerset, but his career then hit a 'glass ceiling' and within three years the club had released him. He turned the ball appreciably, but variations that might have taken him further in the game were lacking; for example, colleagues recall that his 'floater' away from the right-hander was not sufficiently well concealed to deceive the best batsmen around the circuit.

Sully moved in 1964 after finding his path into Somerset's first team blocked by Brian Langford. He made only a dozen appearances for them, spread over four years, and at the age of twenty-four headed to Wantage Road. His patience was put to the test again as Malcolm Scott and Peter Watts bowled most of Northamptonshire's spin in the 1964 Championship season, leaving Sully to claim 74 wickets for the Second XI – still a County record.

Sully broke into Keith Andrew's side in 1965, and in three successive matches during August – against Nottinghamshire, Kent and Lancashire – he snapped up 27 wickets at less than 12 runs apiece. Had he played in the following game at Worcester, which turned out to be the Championship decider and which the home side won comfortably with spinners Norman Gifford and Doug Slade doing the second innings damage, the pennant might conceivably have finished up elsewhere. In the event, Sully was the man to make way for the returning David Larter, leaving Scott to soldier on with inadequate slow-bowling support. Another of cricket's countless 'if onlys'.

In 1966, Sully became the first off-spinner since Vallance Jupp to take 100 wickets in a season for Northamptonshire. He demolished Sussex with 7-29 at Hove, followed up with 7-69 against Essex at Clacton, and received his County cap in August. He was again a major force in 1967 with 80 wickets, but his victims were becoming ever more costly and 1969 found both Sully and left-arm Scott drifting out of favour. Neither was retained at the end of the year, Sully returning to the West Country to ply his trade with Devon in Minor Counties cricket.

Paul Taylor
LHB and LFM, 1991-

Born: Ashby-de-la-Zouch, Leics,
8 August 1964

Batting Career:

M	I	NO	Runs	HS
157	179	56	1,882	86
181	*66*	*34*	*326*	*20*
Ave	**100**	**50**	**ct/st**	
15.30	-	8	53	
10.19	*-*	*-*	*40*	

Bowling Career:

Runs	Wkts	Ave
14,142	502	28.17
6,101	*215*	*28.38*
BB	**5wi**	**10wm**
7-23	17	4
5-45	*1*	*-*

During the summer of 2000, Paul Taylor experienced the extreme ups and downs of a county cricketer's life. With the simultaneous burden and opportunity of a benefit to occupy his thoughts, he suffered an early-season injury which, although allowing him more time for the paperwork, threatened his longer-term prospects as a front-line fast bowler. His first Championship appearance was delayed until the end of July, and he managed only three wickets in as many games.

Then, happily, the clouds rolled away. He returned match figures of 10-69 in a remarkable victory at Eastbourne, delighted himself and his captain by capturing two vital Gloucestershire wickets at Northampton with left-arm spin by way of variety, and joined Northamptonshire's elite by reaching 500 first-class wickets for the club, becoming only the sixteenth man to achieve the feat. Not bad for a player on the cricketing scrapheap a decade earlier.

Rejected by Derbyshire after just seven first-team outings in three years, Taylor eventually found his way into Minor Counties cricket with Staffordshire, who drew Northamptonshire in the first round of the 1990 NatWest Trophy. He 'travelled' to the tune of 92 runs in his 12-over stint, but Wantage Road officials were sufficiently impressed to offer him a contract and a chance to resurrect his career. He proved a revelation in 1992, picking up 68 wickets including four in an over against Hampshire at Bournemouth on his way to 7-23 – a magnificent piece of left-arm swing bowling. His immediate rewards were a player of the year accolade, a County cap and a Test debut in Calcutta.

Taylor's experiences in the England set-up might have left a less equable character feeling, at best, a little bitter, but he buckled down again with Northamptonshire and topped 50 wickets in four successive seasons between 1995 and 1998. He also contributed some handy runs, and no one was more mortified than Taylor himself when, having got to 86 as nightwatchman against Durham in 1995, with a first-class century there for the taking, he holed out. He remains a popular figure with supporters and, by accepting a new one-year contract for 2001, indicated his continuing enthusiasm for the county circuit.

Albert Thomas

RHB and RFM, 1919-33

Born: Ruthin, Denbighshire, 7 June 1893
Died: Kidderminster, 21 March 1965

Batting Career:

M	I	NO	Runs	HS
284	462	103	4,747	84
Ave	**100**	**50**	**ct/st**	
13.22	-	10	120	

Bowling Career:

Runs	Wkts	Ave
20,899	817	25.58
BB	**5wi**	**10wm**
9-30	29	5

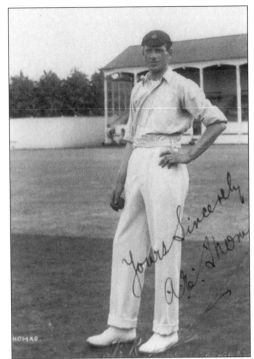

Albert 'Taffy' Thomas delivered more than 63,000 balls for Northamptonshire, the vast majority of them 'on the spot.' Opposing batsmen scored off the medium-pacer from North Wales at an average of just under two runs an over, and his remarkable control was a significant feature of the County's attack in the seasons following the First World War. Furthermore, his approach to life mirrored his approach to cricket: sound, level-headed and a calming influence on some of his more temperamental colleagues.

Billeted in Northampton during the war years, Thomas had attracted the attention of groundsman Alf Stockwin when he came to bowl in the nets at Wantage Road. His debut, against the Australian Imperial Forces side in 1919, was not a great success, but Northampton Grammar School took him on as groundsman and coach, giving Northamptonshire the opportunity to keep tabs on him. They decided to take another look, and he justified their interest with 9-30 against Yorkshire at Bradford in 1920. The last seven wickets cost him six runs, and one lifting ball hit wicketkeeper Walter Buswell in the eye and put him out of the match. Only 'Bumper' Wells' dismissal of Roy Kilner prevented the County's first all-ten.

His place secure, Thomas proceeded to record some staggering analyses over the next decade. In 1926, against Leicestershire at Aylestone Road, he took 2-42 from 45 overs; and that was a costly effort compared to his 3-17 from 34 overs, including 23 maidens, on the same ground in 1930. That same season saw him earn himself a £2 bonus from the Mayor of Northampton after he and Vallance Jupp skittled Bill Woodfull's Australians, Bradman and all, for 93 and made them follow on. Another touring side to fall foul of him were the 1924 South Africans, against whom he claimed 8-96, and Thomas represented the Players against the Gentlemen at Lord's in 1928.

An elbow injury, which necessitated surgery, ended his County career in 1933. He was granted a testimonial which didn't amount to much, and turned to the Birmingham League where he sent down many more maidens for Kidderminster, Aston Unity and Old Hill before putting away his boots in 1948.

George Thompson
RHB and RFM, 1895-1922

Born: Northampton, 27 October 1877				
Died: Bristol, 3 March 1943				
Batting Career:				
M	**I**	**NO**	**Runs**	**HS**
222	392	39	8,321	131*
(114	*165*	*24*	*5,176*	*186*)*
Ave	**100**	**50**	**ct/st**	
23.57	7	40	194	
(36.71	*9*	*26*	*91)*	
Bowling Career:				
Runs	**Wkts**	**Ave**		
20,355	1,078	18.88		
(10,536	*751*	*14.03)*		
BB	**5wi**	**10wm**		
9-64	102	31		
(9-45	*79*	*26)*		

When members and visitors sit down to their lunch in the George Thompson Suite at the County Ground before enjoying an afternoon's cricket featuring the top players from home and overseas, they would do well to remember for a moment the man whose name it bears. There is no excuse not to, for a plaque on the wall says it all: 'To him largely belonged the credit of raising Northamptonshire to the first-class in 1905, and he was recognised as the greatest player the county has ever produced.'

That last word is important. The all-rounder who batted and bowled Northamptonshire into the cricketing big time was not an imported mercenary but a genuine, copper-bottomed local hero, born in Northampton's Louise Road – a well-timed straight drive away from the Racecourse which staged the club's home matches before 1886 – and brought up at 'The Elms' in the village of Cogenhoe. In 1898 it was widely reported that Thompson would be qualifying to play for Kent or possibly Worcestershire; he decided in the end to stay put, unwilling to uproot himself and his wife-to-be (Charlotte, a Cogenhoe girl) from their Northamptonshire home. This despite a prospective mother-in-law who, undertaking a rare visit to the County Ground and seeing the umpires walk out, felt obliged to ask what those two butchers were doing.

Thompson was sent to Wellingborough School shortly after the early death of his mother, and developed the qualities of resilience, self-reliance and determination that were to stand him in good stead on the cricket field. He made his Northamptonshire debut as an amateur in 1895, having been apprenticed to a vet who went bankrupt; he needed a source of income and the County, mindful of the young man's burgeoning talent (he had bagged 9-35 on one of his early appearances, against Buckinghamshire at Wolverton), took him on as assistant-secretary at an annual salary of £75. He turned professional two years later, and proceeded to sweep aside Northamptonshire's opponents in the Second-Class Counties competition for the next nine seasons.

As a batsman he was solid rather than swashbuckling, while his bowling – brisk medium-fast with a high, windmilling action off a shortish run – brought him more than 1,800 wickets for Northamptonshire either side of promotion in 1905. For most of the time, the reliable, accurate Billy East was trundling away at the other end. Captaining the team was easy,

Left: *George Thompson, as drawn by A. Chevalier Tayler.* Right: *Thompson poses for the photographer in around 1905, having batted and bowled Northamptonshire into first-class cricket.*

said Tom Horton: 'I start off with Thompson and East, then switch to East and Thompson!' Inevitably, the newspapers began to talk of 'Thompsonshire' and they had a point. It was entirely appropriate, having helped Northamptonshire to the 'minors' title in both 1903 and 1904, that he should face the County's opening delivery in first-class cricket at Southampton the following season.

Although the batsmen of Yorkshire and Surrey tended to offer rather stiffer resistance than their Berkshire or Wiltshire counterparts had done, Thompson exceeded 100 wickets in seven of the eight years between 1906 and 1913. His time as an MCC ground bowler, a role he combined successfully with Northamptonshire duties, made his name known beyond the county's boundaries, and in 1909 he was picked in the England team to play Australia in the First Test at Edgbaston. In the event, it was a walk-on part: going in at number ten and bowling only four overs. But he appeared in all five Tests in South Africa that winter, finishing second to Jack Hobbs in the batting averages

and taking 23 wickets.

Thompson fell seriously ill in 1918, having served with the Royal Garrison Artillery in the war, and was left with osteomyelitis in his right ankle. He returned to the Northamptonshire side in 1921 and 1922, more perhaps as a talisman than anything else although he made some useful runs. After confirming his retirement he briefly renewed his acquaintance with South Africa, and umpired two of England's Tests out there in 1922/23; Frank Mann's team included Northamptonshire's newly-appointed player-secretary, Vallance Jupp.

Thompson spent most of his remaining years in Bristol, coaching the boys at Clifton College and still sending a few down in the nets. He once told his son, George junior: 'Don't look down on anyone's job as long as what they are doing is honest.' Few county cricketers have put in an honest day's work for their team more often than George Joseph Thompson, and to borrow Sir Christopher Wren's epitaph – 'If you would see his monument, look around.'

Jack Timms

RHB and RM, 1925-49

Born: Silverstone, Northants,
3 November 1906
Died: Buckingham, 18 May 1980
Batting Career:

M	I	NO	Runs	HS
468	842	29	20,384	213
Ave	**100**	**50**	**ct/st**	
25.07	31	102	150	

Bowling Career:

Runs	Wkts	Ave
6,618	149	44.41
BB	**5wi**	**10wm**
6-18	2	-

The lengthy first-class career of Jack Timms began in an optimistic summer for Northamptonshire, 1925, and ended in another, 1949. There were many thoroughly miserable ones in-between. But this good and faithful servant of the club was always doing his level best to lift the gloom with a few runs, a much-needed wicket, a sharp run-out – or a cheery tune from his regular companion on away trips, a portable gramophone.

Like his fellow Old Wellingburian, George Thompson, Timms started out as an amateur and subsequently turned professional. He made his debut in May 1925, aged eighteen, and came through an early test of temperament with flying colours. Against Worcestershire at Kidderminster, the County needed 301 to win and looked out of the reckoning at 92-5 when young Jack came in to join his namesake, Wilfrid Timms. The pair put on 140, the newcomer hitting 72, and Northamptonshire squeezed home by one wicket with the captain, Maurice Fitzroy, unable to bring himself to watch. At least one national newspaper waxed lyrical about 'the Timms brothers' although they were, in fact,

unrelated. This nerve-shredding experience may have had a lasting effect on Jack Timms; colleagues remember him as a reluctant watcher of the match in progress.

His cricketing roots were deep in Northamptonshire soil. His grandfather had been a big noise in the local game as early as the 1860s, and his father served on the County committee. Timms crossed the great divide from the 'unpaid' to the 'paid' in 1927, and the following season reached 1,000 runs for the first time including a maiden Championship century against Glamorgan.

His batting form and oustanding work in the field – 'a not unworthy successor to the great Fanny Walden' in the covers, according to *Wisden* – attracted the attention of the selectors, who handed him the opportunity to stake a claim for international honours in the 1932 Test trial between North and South at Old Trafford. Scores of 5 and 3 ensured it was the closest he ever came to the England side. He settled back into the county routine and enjoyed his most successful summer with the bat in 1934, logging 1,632 runs with a career-best 213 off the Worcestershire bowlers at Stourbridge.

In modern-day parlance, Timms was a 'positive' player. A brave hooker, he would take on the quicker bowlers and showed,

Jack Timms graduated from promising schoolboy to senior professional between 1925 and 1949 – for much of the time with musical accompaniment!

according to R.C. Robertson-Glasgow, 'a generous and cavalier manner of batting, as if conscious but contemptuous of responsibility.' As the dismal 1930s wore on, Northamptonshire were grateful for a top-order man willing and able to mount a counter-attack, even if he didn't always prevail. He also proved a handy change bowler and captured 6-18 at Worcester in 1938, nearly paving the way for Northamptonshire's first Championship victory since Taunton in 1935. When the 'lean spell' (as the *Chronicle and Echo* termed it, not going overboard) ended a year later, against Leicestershire at Northampton, Timms did his bit with a half-century and the wicket of George Dawkes.

He was in harness again after the war, finding his touch immediately with 126 at Lord's in the opening match of the 1946 campaign. As senior pro, it fell to him to convey dressing room concerns about the leadership of Peter Murray-Willis to the committee, who duly switched captains in mid-season and appointed Jack Webster. The man put in charge in 1947, Arthur Childs-Clarke, reported that Timms 'was as audacious as ever' in the summer of Compton and Edrich, and he again passed the 1,000 run mark.

But this was to be his last hurrah. Timms lost form altogether the next season – not the ideal prelude to his testimonial year – and in September 1949, pushing forty-three, he informed the club that he was not interested in a new contract. He had at least written his name in the record books during his final summer, becoming the first man to reach 20,000 runs for Northamptonshire. His achievement in notching up two centuries in the match against Sussex at Kettering in 1939 was also a County first. After his retirement, Timms combined two sporting interests as assistant at Buckingham Golf Club and cricket coach at Bloxham School.

Wilfrid Timms

RHB, 1921-32

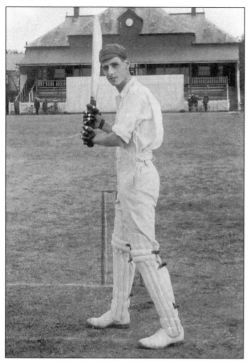

Born: Northampton, 28 September 1902
Died: Godalming, Surrey, 30 September 1986
Batting Career:

M	I	NO	Runs	HS
99	183	14	3,855	154*
Ave	100	50	ct/st	
22.81	4	21	23	

Bowling Career:

Runs	Wkts	Ave	
151	0	-	
BB	5wi	10wm	
-	-	-	

It was a story straight out of the *Boy's Own Paper*. Wilfrid Timms, an eighteen-year-old schoolboy whose family home in Clarke Road overlooked the County Ground, went out to bat for Northamptonshire with the side in deep trouble; following on 381 runs behind they had already lost a second-innings wicket, and the other opener, 'Dick' Woolley, was injured. Timms, batting in his school cap, proceeded to keep Essex at bay throughout the final day's play, and was carried off the field shoulder-high by his chums with an unbeaten 154 to his name. The governors of Northampton Grammar School, delighted at his achievement, granted all the pupils an extra day's holiday.

The game after his Essex triumph was against Warwick Armstrong's Australians, but it clashed with his Cambridge entrance exams; he thus missed the crushing defeat by an innings and 484 runs. Later in the season, however, he captained the County twice, as the 'senior' amateur present in terms of appearances. George Thompson – who was 'genial and amusing' according to Timms –

nursed him through the experience.

He missed out on a blue at Cambridge, and embarked on a teaching career which meant he was unable to play first-class cricket regularly. That was a great shame for Northamptonshire, as his solid technique and temperament earned him further centuries against Worcestershire at Kidderminster in 1925, helping the side to a one-wicket win, and two in 1926, against Warwickshire and Leicestershire.

When, a couple of years later, he tackled Harold Larwood by giving himself room to play the lifting deliveries on the off side, his captain, Vallance Jupp, called the quiet, scholarly Timms 'a bloody coward.' Jupp suggested publicly that the same was true of Don Bradman during the 1932/33 'Bodyline' series.

Timms went on to teach languages at Charterhouse, where he also ran the school's cricket between 1932 and 1946. One of his star pupils was Peter May, who paid tribute to his old mentor: 'He was always very patient and encouraging; we valued his advice because he had been successful himself in county cricket.' In retirement, Timms remained close to Charterhouse and would from time to time glance through the sheaf of letters and telegrams received in the aftermath of his 1921 brush with fame.

George Tribe

LHB and SLA, 1951-59

Born: Yarraville, Melbourne, Australia, 4 October 1920				
Batting Career:				
M	I	NO	Runs	HS
233	356	67	8,141	136*
Ave	100	50	ct/st	
28.16	6	39	181	
Bowling Career:				
Runs	Wkts	Ave		
20,681	1,021	20.25		
BB	5wi	10wm		
9-43	71	13		

Statistics, they say, can prove anything. They don't, however, require a great deal of manipulation to support the contention that George Tribe was Northamptonshire's most successful all-rounder, at least (in deference to George Thompson) since first-class status was achieved. The ever-enthusiastic Australian, who baffled batsmen with his myriad of left-arm 'back of the hand' variations – chinamen, top-spinners, throw it up, push it through – and contributed vital runs from number seven or thereabouts, played eight full seasons with the County between 1952 and 1959 and did the 'double' in seven of them, only falling short in the wet summer of 1958 when he managed just 722 runs to set against his 110 wickets.

The irresistible combination of Jock Livingston and British Timken brought Tribe to the County Ground. He had played in three Tests against Wally Hammond's England side in 1946/47 and helped Victoria to the Sheffield Shield that season, but spin was not figuring high on the agenda of the Australian selectors at the time and he came to England to earn a living in the Central Lancashire League. As the best man at Livingston's wedding, there was a ready-made link; negotiations with Northamptonshire were successfully concluded towards the end

of 1950. His debut the following June, while completing his qualifying period, whetted the appetite in a big way. Tribe took 6-53 to force the South Africans to follow on, and the stage was set for his first Championship campaign in 1952.

That effort against the tourists was no flash in the pan. Against Nottinghamshire at Trent Bridge he dismissed John Clay, caught behind by Ken Fiddling, with his opening delivery in the three-day competition. He claimed 11-119 there, 12-133 at Horsham two games later, and by the end of his fourth Championship match had 40 wickets to his credit. It set the tone for the rest of the decade.

Tribe reserved some of his most devastating performances for Yorkshire. Traditionally suspect against wrist-spin, their batsmen pushed and prodded without ever quite working out what day of the week it was. At Bradford in 1954 he snapped up a dozen victims in the game, only to finish on the losing side; a year on, also at Park Avenue, he was even more destructive with 6-30 and 9-45, and Northamptonshire lost again. But the result was

What's coming this time? Another baffling delivery from George Tribe, who performed the 'double' seven times in eight seasons.

altogether more palatable at a decidedly damp Wantage Road in July 1958 – Tribe took 7-22 in the first innings and 8-9, those wickets coming in the space of 24 balls, in the second. Victory followed between the showers.

Three weeks later he recorded his second nine-wicket haul for the County, destroying Worcestershire with 9-43 in Dennis Brookes' benefit match. Freddie Brown wrote that Tribe 'was always at his best when the match was closest.' But when he was at his best, the matches were often not very close at all.

His haul of 175 wickets in 1955 is likely to stand as a Northamptonshire record for the foreseeable future; no-one else has ever managed even 150. His benefit in 1956 raised £2,695 – a respectable sum at the time – and he showed his gratitude with another 127

scalps in 1957 to help the County to second place in the table.

To add to his prodigious bowling feats – and Brown always maintained he would have been more successful still, given quicker pitches than were the norm at Northampton in the 1950s – Tribe also registered six centuries, including a gritty effort against Lancashire at Rushden in 1959, his 'farewell' summer. He had come to terms early on with the rigours of six days a week county cricket, but towards the end of 1958 informed the Northamptonshire committee that he didn't intend to carry on at the end of his present contract. Efforts to persuade him to stay on failed and he retired at the same time as Brookes, receiving a teaset for his trouble. It was, truly, the end of an era.

Frank Tyson

RHB and RF, 1952-60

Born: Farnworth, Lancs, 6 June 1930

Batting Career:

M	I	NO	Runs	HS
170	218	54	2,842	82
Ave	**100**	**50**	**ct/st**	
17.32	-	9	66	

Bowling Career:

Runs	Wkts	Ave
10,998	525	20.94
BB	**5wi**	**10wm**
8-60	25	3

Not many Northamptonshire players have had a calypso written in their honour; fewer still have appeared in an episode of *Hancock's Half Hour*. But Frank 'Typhoon' Tyson attained national, and indeed international, celebrity by dint of his performances on England's successful Ashes expedition of 1954/55. His record for the County is also highly impressive, and would have been even better had the pitches at Wantage Road in the 1950s been more conducive to genuine pace.

Tyson represented another 'scoop' for Jock Livingston. The pair were in opposition one Sunday afternoon at Kypersley in the Potteries; Tyson, a Lancastrian whose senior cricket began as a teenager at Middleton, now a university student and part-time professional, representing the North Staffordshire League against a Commonwealth team containing Livingston. The Australian liked what he saw, invited Tyson for a trial early in 1952, and by June he had signed.

His first-class debut, against the Indians at the County Ground, must have attracted a crowd well into six figures – at least, if all those who have since claimed to be present actually were. Tyson's sensational first over forced the slips back several yards and his sixth ball had Pankaj Roy caught behind by (a good quiz question, this) Brian Reynolds. The over was, according to captain Freddie Brown, 'the fastest I have seen by an English bowler since Harold Larwood bowled in Australia in 1932/33.' A year later the Aussies visited Northampton, and Tyson was at it again. His second delivery of the innings trapped Colin McDonald leg-before – painfully so – and his fourth accounted for Graeme Hole, played on. Brown, an England selector by this time, was loving every minute of it.

Tyson played a full season for the first time in 1954, claiming 78 wickets in all matches include five in the final Test of the summer against Pakistan at The Oval. He and Keith Andrew were both chosen in Len Hutton's touring party to head Down Under in September, and there was even talk of a civic reception in Northampton until the County committee deemed the suggestion 'unbalanced and unnecessary.' Before the year was out, they were probably thinking rather differently. Operating off a shortened run, Tyson helped England square the series with ten wickets in the Second Test at Sydney; then in Melbourne he claimed 7-27

Frank Tyson bowling, towards the end of his career. In modern sporting parlance, he was the ultimate 'impact player' in the early 1950s.

as Australia collapsed in their second innings and lost again. Hutton's men took the series 3-1, and in those three victories 'Typhoon' blew away 25 batsmen.

He went to Australia and New Zealand again with Peter May in 1958/59, bringing down the curtain on a Test career that brought Tyson 76 wickets in 17 games. By then he was battling against injury, but could still be a serious threat on his day. Crowds away from Northampton saw the best of him; in 1957, a summer dominated from the County's point of view by the trio of left-arm spinners, he bagged a match haul of 13-112 to set up a victory over Surrey at The Oval, and demolished Glamorgan with 7-25 in the second innings at Cardiff Arms Park.

Frank Tyson's brief and brilliant stay in first-class cricket ended with his retirement in 1960, but not before he had furnished the County Ground faithful with one more memorable tourist game moment. Needing 200 in 165 minutes to beat the South Africans that summer, Northamptonshire got there by four wickets thanks in part to Tyson's knock of 29 in 14 minutes, featuring 3 sixes and 2 fours. He could bat a bit, too.

Tyson emigrated to Australia, the scene of his greatest triumphs, and has been a respected schoolmaster, coach, commentator and writer. An erudite and cultured man, whose well-informed opinions on fast bowling are still sought today, his lasting affection for the County is evident: 'Many … have undoubtedly been better cricketers than me. They have probably made more money than me out of cricket. But not one player has derived more enjoyment than me out of Northants cricket.' And this is in spite of those pitches…

Born: Northampton, 18 March 1887				
Died: Northampton, 26 April 1974				
Batting Career:				
M	I	NO	Runs	HS
122	220	10	3,808	129
(8	*11*	*2*	*286*	*93)*
Ave	100	50	ct/st	
18.13	2	14	105	
(31.78	*-*	*2*	*-)*	
Bowling Career:				
Runs	Wkts	Ave		
19	0	-		
BB	5wi	10wm		
-	-	-		

'Tubby' Vials – the nickname supposedly stemmed from a schoolboy exploit involving a tub – might easily have gone down in history as the first captain to lead Northamptonshire to the County Championship title. He missed out by a whisker in 1912. As it was, he became a 'heart and soul' figure at the centre of the club's affairs, serving in various key capacities until 1968 when he stood down after twelve years as president.

The son of Thomas Henry Vials, the club's honorary secretary between 1883 and 1891, 'Tubby' (christened George Alfred Turner) succeeded 'Tim' Manning as skipper in 1911, and the following year nearly pulled off one of the most sensational triumphs in Championship history. Using only twelve players in 18 matches, Northamptonshire finished the campaign with 70.58 per cent of their possible points against Yorkshire's 72 per cent. Rain on 7 August prevented the County polishing off Leicestershire, and saved the Tykes from probable defeat in the Roses game at Old Trafford – if only! Vials himself added a dash of glamour to proceedings by flaying Surrey's bowlers for 82 in 70 minutes at Northampton to set up victory; the reason for his hurry, he explained years later, was a friend's wedding the next morning.

Vials had made his Northamptonshire debut as a seventeen-year-old, against Staffordshire in May 1904. He scored 48 batting at number eight, and quickly worked his way up the order. He trained and qualified as a solicitor, limiting his county cricket, but still made some important runs including a century at Yorkshire's expense in 1910 when the County beat them for the first time. The Bramall Lane crowd couldn't quite understand what was going off out there. Knee trouble further abbreviated his career – a one-off appearance in 1922 notwithstanding – but he joined the committee before the First World War and remained closely involved.

Having chaired the selection comittee either side of the Second World War, he graduated to become chairman of the club between 1951 and his election to the presidency in 1956. His death, just as the 1974 cricket season was getting underway, left Billy Denton as the last survivor of Northamptonshire's glorious class of 1912.

Roy Virgin

RHB, 1973-77

Born: Taunton, 26 August 1939				
Batting Career:				
M	**I**	**NO**	**Runs**	**HS**
103	184	14	5,703	145
86	*80*	*2*	*1,817*	*82*
Ave	**100**	**50**	**ct/st**	
33.54	13	28	101	
23.29	*-*	*14*	*31*	
Bowling Career:				
Runs	**Wkts**	**Ave**		
19	0	-		
4	*0*	*-*		
BB	**5wi**	**10wm**		
-	-	-		
-	-	-		

Although a Northamptonshire player for only four-and-a-half seasons, Roy Virgin has joined the ranks of those ex-professional cricketers prepared to put something back into the game. He joined the club's committee in 1990, and has served since 1997 as chairman of the influential cricket sub-committee, following Peter Arnold and Roy Wills into the post.

Taunton born and bred, Virgin appeared for Somerset from 1957 to 1972. In 1970 he topped 2,000 runs and was talked of as a possible for Ray Illingworth's Ashes expedition, but just two years later, in the wake of a wretched summer with the bat, he moved to Northampton. The registration rules prevented him playing before 1 July 1973, and he took some time to settle into his new cricketing environment. Having done so, he flourished in 1974 with 1,936 runs including 7 centuries – just one short of Bob Haywood's long-standing record. The next-highest aggregate was Jim Watts' 1,040, and Virgin also made a big difference in the field, proving one of the safest slip catchers on the circuit. This was especially helpful as Northamptonshire were at last able to boast a bowling attack worthy of the name.

Before that season was over, the club had settled on Virgin to succeed Watts as captain for 1975. With David Steele not keen to take on the job in his benefit year, the experienced opening batsman became the obvious choice. He presided over a depressing start to what would become 'The Summer of Steele', and after Mike Brearley's unbeaten 118 steered Middlesex home in a run-chase at the County Ground at the end of July, Northamptonshire's sixth defeat of the Championship campaign, Virgin's reign ended by mutual consent.

Relieved of the burden, he regained his own batting form in 1976, and his knocks of 82 and 53 in the semi-final and final were decisive factors in the Gillette Cup triumph. He left the first-class game at the end of 1977 and concentrated on business before offering his knowledge and energy to the committee 'pool', eventually forming a cordial working relationship with Bob Carter and Matthew Hayden which paid handsome dividends in 2000.

Fred 'Fanny' Walden

RHB and RM, 1910-29

Born: Wellingborough, 1 March 1888
Died: Northampton, 3 May 1949
Batting Career:

M	I	NO	Runs	HS
258	435	36	7,462	128
Ave	**100**	**50**	**ct/st**	
18.70	5	26	131	

Bowling Career:

Runs	Wkts	Ave
4,228	114	37.08
BB	**5wi**	**10wm**
4-39	-	-

A cricketer and footballer of considerable repute, 'Fanny' Walden (the nickname derived, apparently, from the lady who kept the corner shop near his boyhood home in Wellingborough) launched his twin sporting careers just before the First World War. He signed for Northampton Town, managed then by Herbert Chapman, in the winter of 1908/09 (later achieving far greater prominence with Tottenham Hotspur, including 2 England caps), and made his first-class debut for Northamptonshire in 1910 as a somewhat rough-hewn middle-order batsman, brilliant fielder and occasional partnership-breaker with the ball.

Walden's record in County colours is modest; he never reached 1,000 runs in a season for Northamptonshire, and managed only 5 centuries in 435 innings. The first of them came against Lancashire in 1919, while the third, off Surrey's bowlers in 1920, was somewhat overshadowed by Percy Fender's 35-minute effort for the opposition. A six-year interval followed before 'Fanny' added a fourth to his tally, and the fifth and last, also in 1926, saw him post 229 for the seventh wicket with Wilfrid Timms against Warwickshire.

But he saved many runs in the covers – at only 5 feet 2 inches he was near the ground to

begin with – and generally provided some much-needed vim and vigour in a side not overburdened with chirpy confidence. He was granted a benefit in 1927 and retired a couple of years later to join the first-class umpires list. Walden rose through the ranks to stand in the first of his 11 Tests in 1934, going on to officiate in some of the most memorable international contests of the period: South Africa's historic victory at Lord's in 1935, Len Hutton's dismal debut against New Zealand in 1937, and then his epic 364 at The Oval the following season.

Walden's umpiring stint ended with the outbreak of war in 1939, and he spent his remaining days working at the now-demolished Peacock Hotel on Northampton's Market Square, with a little cricket coaching at the town's Grammar School. He died at the age of sixty-one, the day before Freddie Brown's 'New Look' Northamptonshire team took the field for the first time at Taunton. He would have enjoyed that summer's results and the manner in which they were achieved, reflecting his own zestful approach.

Jim Watts
LHB and RM, 1959-80

Born: Henlow, Beds, 16 June 1940
Batting Career:

M	I	NO	Runs	HS
372	605	90	14,411	145
151	*126*	*14*	*1,845*	*83*
Ave	**100**	**50**	**ct/st**	
27.98	10	75	278	
16.47	*-*	*3*	*59*	

Bowling Career:

Runs	Wkts	Ave
8,613	331	26.02
3,081	*117*	*26.33*
BB	**5wi**	**10wm**
6-18	7	-
5-24	*1*	*-*

When Northamptonshire bestowed the grand-sounding title of 'Cricketer Emeritus' on half a dozen distinguished former players in 1999, it was entirely appropriate that Jim Watts should be among them. He may never have scaled the dizziest heights as an all-rounder, but his value extended far beyond that of just another solid, workaday county pro. Twice he took on the captaincy in very difficult circumstances, and twice he left the side in an immeasurably better state than he had found it.

In the autumn of 1970, Northamptonshire faced the future without the services of Roger Prideaux, Brian Reynolds and Albert Lightfoot, and with Mushtaq Mohammad expected to miss a good part of the following summer on tour with Pakistan. Watts, only back at Wantage Road for a season after three years out of the county game, was the committee's unanimous choice to take charge. Boosted by Mushtaq's availability for all but the Tests against England, Watts' men regrouped in 1971; high-quality cricketers were recruited to bolster the staff; and Northamptonshire finished fourth, third and

third again in the Championship before Watts handed over the baton to concentrate on his teaching career.

It was given back to him, briefly, in August 1975 when Roy Virgin's reign ended after three months. Watts promptly broke a finger and Mushtaq inherited the job. But he received the call again at the end of 1977 with the club in turmoil as the committee crossed swords with several key players, including the outgoing captain. At the subsequent Extraordinary General Meeting, held just before Christmas, Watts took his place on the platform to face the members, some of whom had formed themselves into an Action Group to demand, at the very least, a full explanation of all the behind-the-scenes machinations.

The atmosphere was still strained as the 1978 season began, but for Watts cricket's importance diminished rapidly as his wife became seriously ill and, tragically, died. He bravely returned to the side in July, and the next two summers saw his Northamptonshire team reach the Gillette Cup final, win the Benson & Hedges Cup (with Watts' tactical acumen seen to best advantage in an absorbing semi-final struggle against Mike Brearley's Middlesex at Lord's), and drag itself off the bottom of the Championship table. When he retired, once and for all, in 1980,

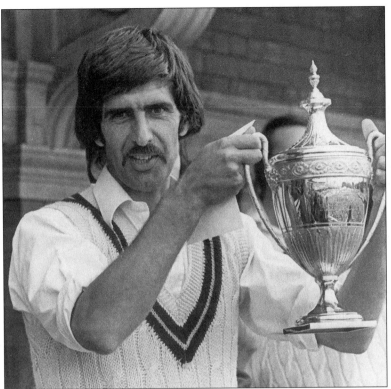

A proud moment – Jim Watts with the Benson & Hedges Cup, 1980.

the Annual Report praised both his leadership – 'of the highest order' – and his 'valuable' personal contributions with bat and ball. That certainly wasn't overstating the case.

The brother of leg-spinner Peter, who notched up 158 County appearances between 1958 and 1966, Jim made his Northamptonshire debut as an eighteen-year-old in 1959, and reached 1,000 runs in each of his first four seasons. He was a significant figure in the 1965 Championship challenge, heading the batting averages with 1,211 runs at 31.05 and picking up 44 wickets. Mindful of both the need to secure a future outside cricket and the possibility that a groin injury might restrict his bowling opportunities, Watts asked to be released in 1966; but he was fit enough to set a new Northants County League record two years later, claiming 10-10 for Rushden against Kettering.

Back in the County fold, he set the standard in 1971 with 1,311 runs, and the following August led Northamptonshire to a hugely satisfying seven-wicket victory over Ian Chappell's Australians. 'The better side won' observed secretary Ken Turner in a tone that brooked no argument. It was, for Watts, 'the greatest moment since I became captain.' Another highlight was the 59-run John Player League triumph over one-day specialists Lancashire in 1974; it was Watts' benefit match, and he marked the occasion with a fluent 61.

He briefly joined the committee after his retirement and ruffled a few feathers with his support for Les Bentley, the head groundsman sacked in 1982 who unsuccessfully took the club to an industrial tribunal alleging unfair dismissal. Watts' formal links with Northamptonshire ended soon afterwards, but his inclusion in that first group of worthies a decade and a half later proved, reassuringly, that his enormous contribution had not been overlooked.

William 'Bumper' Wells

RHB and RFM, 1904-1926

Born: Daventry, 14 March 1881
Died: Daventry, 18 March 1939
Batting Career:

M	I	NO	Runs	HS
269	441	75	6,324	119
(2	3	1	20	13)
Ave	**100**	**50**	**ct/st**	
17.27	2	24	114	
(10.00	-	-	4)	

Bowling Career:

Runs	Wkts	Ave
16,202	751	21.57
(101	2	50.50
BB	**5wi**	**10wm**
8-35	51	10
-	-	-

Legend has it that 'Bumper' Wells owed his professional cricket career to an officer in the Northamptonshire Regiment who spotted him taking wickets in military matches out in South Africa. Wells' name was passed on to the County committee, who also liked the look of the strapping young fellow from Daventry, and he made his debut against Staffordshire at Stoke in 1904.

His approach was uncomplicated but effective, and it says much for his physical strength that he was still undoing batsmen with pace and bounce in his mid-forties. He established himself as a regular in 1908, and apart from his 75 wickets he also demonstrated a degree of batting talent – against Lancashire at the County Ground, he and fellow fast bowler Dave Hardy scored an unbroken 23 for the last wicket to earn a frantic first-ever victory over the red rose county.

Wells got himself into trouble with the club in 1909 when, along with a number of other pros, he objected to being required to bowl longer hours in the nets at the same rate of pay. The rebels refused to sign the attendance book, were duly suspended, and it took the intervention of Charlie Pool, an amateur respected by all, to bring about a truce.

He enjoyed life but, as Jim Coldham euphemistically put it, 'suffered from the fast bowler's traditional failing for pints.' It is somehow not a surprise to discover that in the midst of the heroic Championship bid of 1912, on the eve of a crucial encounter with Surrey, dear old 'Bumper' turned out for the Licensed Traders of Northampton and claimed 7-16 in a convivial match described as 'a great success as a social function.'

Ale consumption notwithstanding, Wells didn't miss a game that season, and returned to pound in again after the First World War when he recorded some of his best figures – including a career-best 8-35 against Yorkshire at Bramall Lane in 1919.

Wells was finally forced to retire in 1926, without a hoped-for 'long service' testimonial, and his declining years were not prosperous. Shortly before his death, after a long illness, he received a £10 grant from the MCC Benevolent Fund. It was a sad end for an endearing Northamptonshire character.

Born: Northampton, 28 November 1962

Batting Career:

M	I	NO	Runs	HS
119	167	21	3,688	144
155	*112*	*31*	*1,483*	*91*
Ave	**100**	**50**	**ct/st**	
25.26	5	13	40	
18.31	*-*	*7*	*34*	

Bowling Career:

Runs	Wkts	Ave
2,910	66	44.09
3,192	*111*	*28.76*
BB	**5wi**	**10wm**
4-4	-	-
5-7	*1*	*-*

As a cricketer with any amount of natural talent who failed to make the hoped-for impact on Northamptonshire's behalf, Duncan Wild belongs fairly and squarely to the 1980s – possibly the club's most frustrating decade.

The son of John Wild, a highly-rated off-spinner who turned out for the County between 1953 and 1961, Duncan was already being talked of as a Northamptonshire star of the future when barely into his teens. His Second XI debut came as a fifteen-year-old in 1978 and he tasted first-class cricket at Cambridge two seasons later, becoming the club's third-youngest player since the war. England Under-19s honours followed, alongside David Capel, and a brace of fine Championship centuries in 1984 – 128 against Kent in the first-ever tie at Northampton, and 144 off Lancashire's bowlers at Southport – convinced many that the fluent left-hander had 'arrived.'

Wild's strokeplaying ability, together with his tidy medium-pace bowling and brilliant fielding, made him an ideal man for the limited-overs competitions. In 1986 he thoroughly enjoyed Northamptonshire's first Sunday League visit to Finedon, claiming 5-7 to secure a big win, and the following year assumed the supporting role in a stirring unbroken partnership with Allan Lamb which earned the side victory in the Benson & Hedges Cup semi-final against Kent at Canterbury. Wild made only 10 out of 68 but, as Lamb recalls, 'Duncan pinned his ears back and ran like a hare.' Ones became twos, twos became threes, and Kent's fielders became thoroughly irritated.

Geoff Cook's decision not to try Wild's gentle seamers in the final against Yorkshire, when other bowlers were proving expensive, was, the captain later admitted, a mistake. He did get on in the NatWest decider against Nottinghamshire later that season, had a catch dropped near the end, and Northamptonshire lost again. In truth, his career had peaked. Championship form and full fitness proved elusive and, towards the end of 1990, he announced his retirement at twenty-seven.

'Oscar' Wild concentrated successfully on business for the next decade – underlining the importance of being earnest – but renewed his involvement with the club by joining the committee in 2000.

Peter Willey

RHB and RM/OB, 1966-83

Born: Sedgefield, Co Durham, 6 December 1949				
Batting Career:				
M	**I**	**NO**	**Runs**	**HS**
319	521	77	13,252	227
264	*253*	*22*	*6,223*	*107*
Ave	**100**	**50**	**ct/st**	
29.84	21	57	129	
26.94	*6*	*37*	*67*	

Bowling Career:		
Runs	**Wkts**	**Ave**
13,981	477	29.31
5,991	*206*	*29.08*
BB	**5wi**	**10wm**
7-37	17	2
4-38	*-*	*-*

That Peter Willey should become one of the world's most respected Test umpires will have surprised no one who followed his playing career closely. He was, and is, a strong man, physically and mentally, and it would be difficult to imagine anyone less likely to buckle meekly under pressure. Just ask the West Indies' pace battery off whom Willey took two Test centuries – at The Oval in 1980 and at St John's, Antigua the following winter. His square-on stance infuriated the purists, but his was a wicket the bowlers always had to earn.

Northamptonshire took Willey on as a fifteen-year-old in 1965, and after a glowing testimonial from Dennis Brookes he made his first-class debut against Cambridge University the following summer at 16 years 180 days – becoming Northamptonshire's second-youngest player after Thomas Welch in 1922. He hit 78 in the second innings, although it was to be five years before he registered a Championship century.

Willey enjoyed the season of his life in 1976. He reached 1,000 County runs for the first time, continued his successful transformation from medium-pacer to off-spinner (a consequence of

serious knee trouble), earned an England call-up for the last two Tests against the West Indies and carried off the Man of the Match award for his knock of 65 in Northamptonshire's Gillette Cup final triumph over Lancashire. He also registered the highest score of his career, 227 off Somerset's bowlers at Wantage Road, and shared in a record-breaking fourth-wicket stand of 370 with Roy Virgin. In 1979 a stirring Gillette semi-final century at Hove took the County to Lord's again, while his bowling came to the fore in the 1980 Benson & Hedges Cup victory over Essex as he captured the key wickets of Mike Denness and Ken McEwan.

Banned from England selection after joining the first 'rebel' tour to South Africa, Willey savaged attacks around the country with 1,783 runs for Northamptonshire in 1982 and 1,546 the year after. But his support, along with Wayne Larkins, for sacked head groundsman Les Bentley at an industrial tribunal was not an action likely to find favour in the committee room. Willey was offered only a one-year contract for 1984, promptly moved to Leicestershire, and stayed there until his retirement in 1991. Happily, his Northampton links were never entirely severed, and local youngsters continue to benefit from his coaching expertise in between umpiring commitments.

Richard Williams

RHB and OB, 1974-92

Born: Bangor, Caernarvonshire, 10 August 1957

Batting Career:

M	I	NO	Runs	HS
278	437	62	11,645	175*
262	*219*	*47*	*4,217*	*94*
Ave	**100**	**50**	**ct/st**	
31.05	18	55	95	
24.52	*-*	*22*	*66*	

Bowling Career:

Runs	Wkts	Ave	
12,526	372	33.67	
4,575	*157*	*29.14*	
BB	**5wi**	**10wm**	
7-73	9	-	
5-30	*1*	*-*	

In some respects, Richard Williams was an 'old fashioned' kind of county cricketer. As an off-spinner, he tested and tempted batsmen with flight and turn rather than firing it in and fighting a war of attrition. On top of this, he remained a Northamptonshire player for the whole of his career, declining to 'do the rounds' in search of an extra few quid. His patience also extended to waiting several seasons for a regular first-team place to come his way, and then doing his damnedest to hang on to it until injury forced his retirement.

Williams was still a month short of his fifteenth birthday when he made his debut for the County's Second XI in 1972, breaking his bat in the process, and he sampled first-class cricket at Oxford (in a losing Northamptonshire side!) in June 1974. A motorcycle accident restricted his early progress, but the 'purge' of 1977 offered opportunities to the young all-rounder, and by the end of the decade he had become one-fifth of 'The Famous Five' at the top of the Northamptonshire order – Cook, Larkins, Williams, Lamb and Willey. 'Chippy' (as a carpenter he handled the renovation of the old 'signal box' at Wantage Road in the 1980s) announced himself with a purple patch in 1979 during which he made 536 runs in seven innings, including 120 against the Indian tourists, and received his County cap.

The following season was even more productive – 1,262 runs and 48 wickets in the first-class game, and a Man of the Match award in Northamptonshire's Benson & Hedges Cup semi-final victory over Middlesex. He attracted the attention of the England selectors, who named him as a reserve for Keith Fletcher's 1981/82 tour to India and Sri Lanka. Test recognition eluded him, but he continued to shine for his county and was voted player of the year in the hectic 'two finals' summer of 1987.

Unfortunately, the beginning of the end came in August 1988 when he wrenched his knee during a century against Essex. Full fitness proved elusive after that, and this doughty professional – almost as adept with hammer, chisel or fishing rod as with a cricket bat – sadly took his leave of the County during the 1992 season.

Claud Woolley

RHB and RM, 1911-31

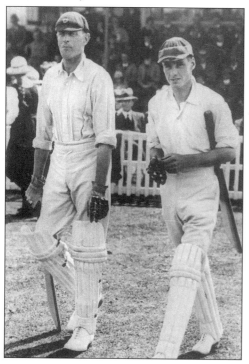

Born: Tonbridge, Kent, 5 May 1886				
Died: Northampton, 3 November 1962				
Batting Career:				
M	**I**	**NO**	**Runs**	**HS**
362	654	33	15,353	204*
Ave	**100**	**50**	**ct/st**	
24.72	13	78	135	

Bowling Career:		
Runs	**Wkts**	**Ave**
11,609	352	32.98
BB	**5wi**	**10wm**
6-30	12	1

During a career spanning twenty years, 'Dick' Woolley possibly fought more rearguard actions on Northamptonshire's behalf than any other batsman in the County's history. While brother Frank delighted the crowds and critics for Kent and England, Claud battled his way to more than 15,000 runs for the Championship's perennial strugglers in the seasons after the First World War. He carried his bat through an innings on three occasions in the 1920s, and was usually required – as Jim Coldham has pointed out – to sacrifice style for safety.

Having made a solitary appearance for Gloucestershire, Woolley worked as the professional at Lilford Hall, seat of the County club's president, until he qualified for Championship cricket with Northamptonshire in 1912. A polished 92 not out at The Oval and his maiden century against Somerset, both in the last summer of peace, attracted some encouraging notices, and when cricket resumed he became a mainstay at the top of the order. He reached 1,000 runs in seven of the nine seasons between 1921 and 1929, taking an unbeaten 204 off Worcestershire's bowlers in the first of those years and notching a career-best 1,602 runs in 1928. Woolley's medium-pace bowling proved an asset too; he performed the hat-trick against Essex in 1920.

Owed £70 in back wages by the club after the 1921 season, he threatened to join Frank at Kent but was talked into staying put, and the following year he earned a game for the Players against the Gentlemen at The Oval, along with his team-mate Vernon Murdin. As senior pro, and in the absence of any available amateur, he captained Northamptonshire to a ten-wicket victory against his native county in 1929.

In the unhappy aftermath of the upheavals that shook the cash-starved club in the autumn of 1931, Woolley was released at the age of forty-five. Had the finances been stronger, he would probably have been appointed coach. As it was, he went on the first-class umpires list and stood with Dai Davies in the Ashes Test at Lord's in 1948. After that, he 'came home' to the County Ground and worked as assistant groundsman to Ron Johnson and Bert Brailsford until shortly before his death.